Voices from Bridge River

The Bridge River Hydroelectric Projects, the People Who Built Them, and the Lives They Touched

Voices from Bridge River

BC Hydro Power Pioneers with Kerry Gold

Figure.1
Vancouver / Toronto / Berkeley

Copyright © 2022 by BC Hydro Power Pioneers

22 23 24 25 5 4 3 2 1

All rights are reserved and no part of this publication may be reproduced, stored in a retrieval system, or transmitted in any form or by any means, electronic, mechanic, photocopying, scanning, recording or otherwise, except as authorized with written permission by the publisher. Excerpts from this publication may be reproduced under licence from Access Copyright.

Cataloguing data is available from Library and Archives Canada
ISBN 978-1-77327-107-1 (pbk.)

Design by Natalie Olsen
Copy editing by Pam Robertson
Proofreading by Renate Preuss
Indexing by Stephen Ullstrom
Front cover photograph by Parry Films, courtesy of BC Hydro Library and Archives
Back cover photographs (clockwise from top left): courtesy of Dave Devitt; courtesy of J.M. Stewart; courtesy of Mike Cleven; courtesy of the Royal BC Museum

Printed and bound in Canada by Friesens

Figure 1 Publishing Inc.
Vancouver BC Canada
www.figure1publishing.com

Figure 1 Publishing is located in the traditional, unceded territory of the xʷməθkʷəy̓əm (Musqueam), Sk̲wx̲wú7mesh (Squamish), and səlilwətaɬ (Tsleil-Waututh) peoples.

This book is dedicated by the BC Hydro Power Pioneers to those who had the vision of a province built on the power of its hydroelectric potential and to the men and women whose hard work, energy and pride built the great electricity system we enjoy today. Our thanks go out to the Indigenous communities and many others who contributed to the story of the development of the Bridge River projects.

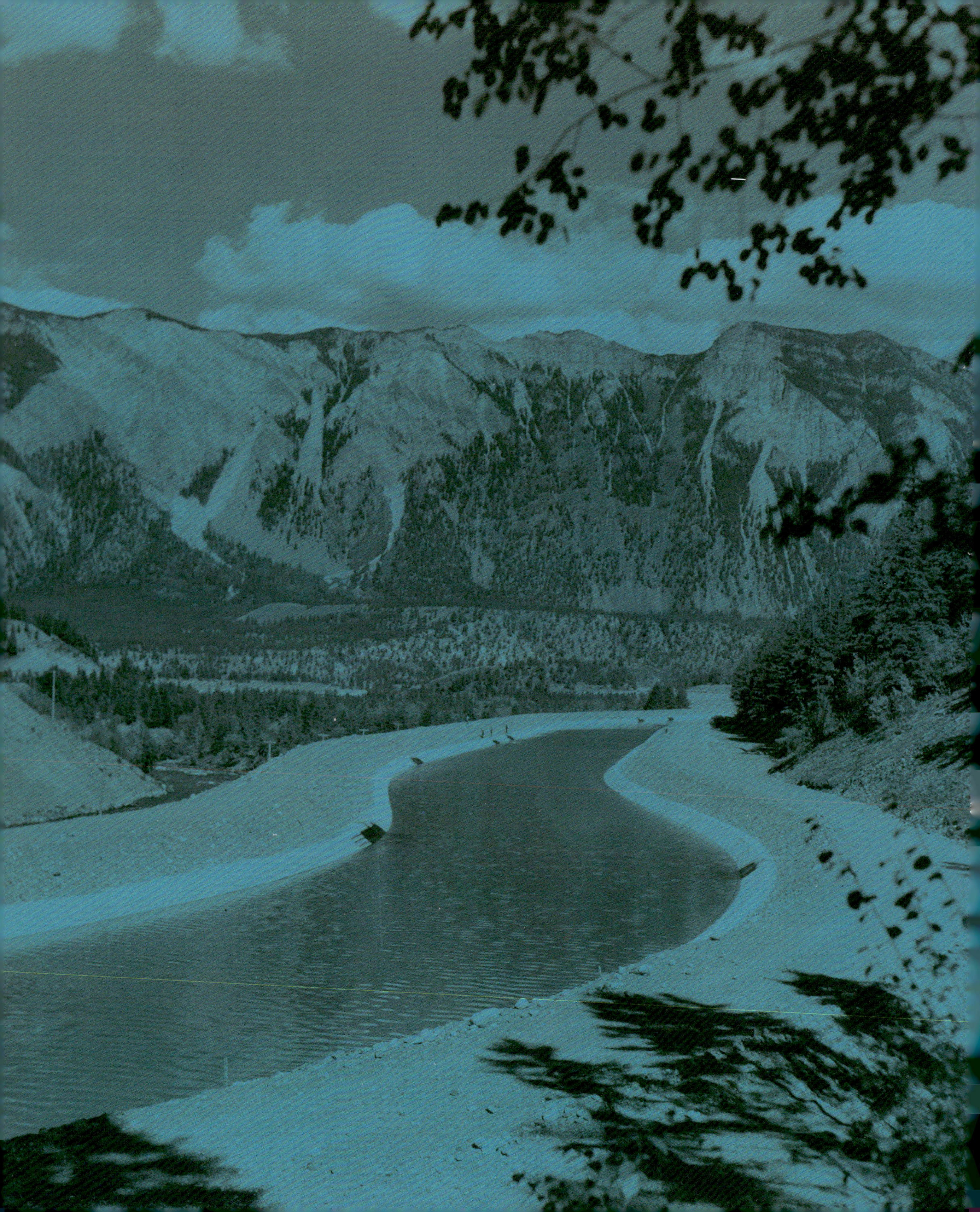

Contents

Introduction ix

1 Potential Power 2

2 Construction Begins 20

3 Valley of Plenty 38

4 Bridge River Internment Camp 52

5 The Construction Era 70

6 Life at the Townsite 124

7 The Impacts 148

8 An Agreement for St'át'imc Reconciliation 166

Epilogue: **A Work in Progress** 175
Acknowledgements 179
Notes 181
Index 183

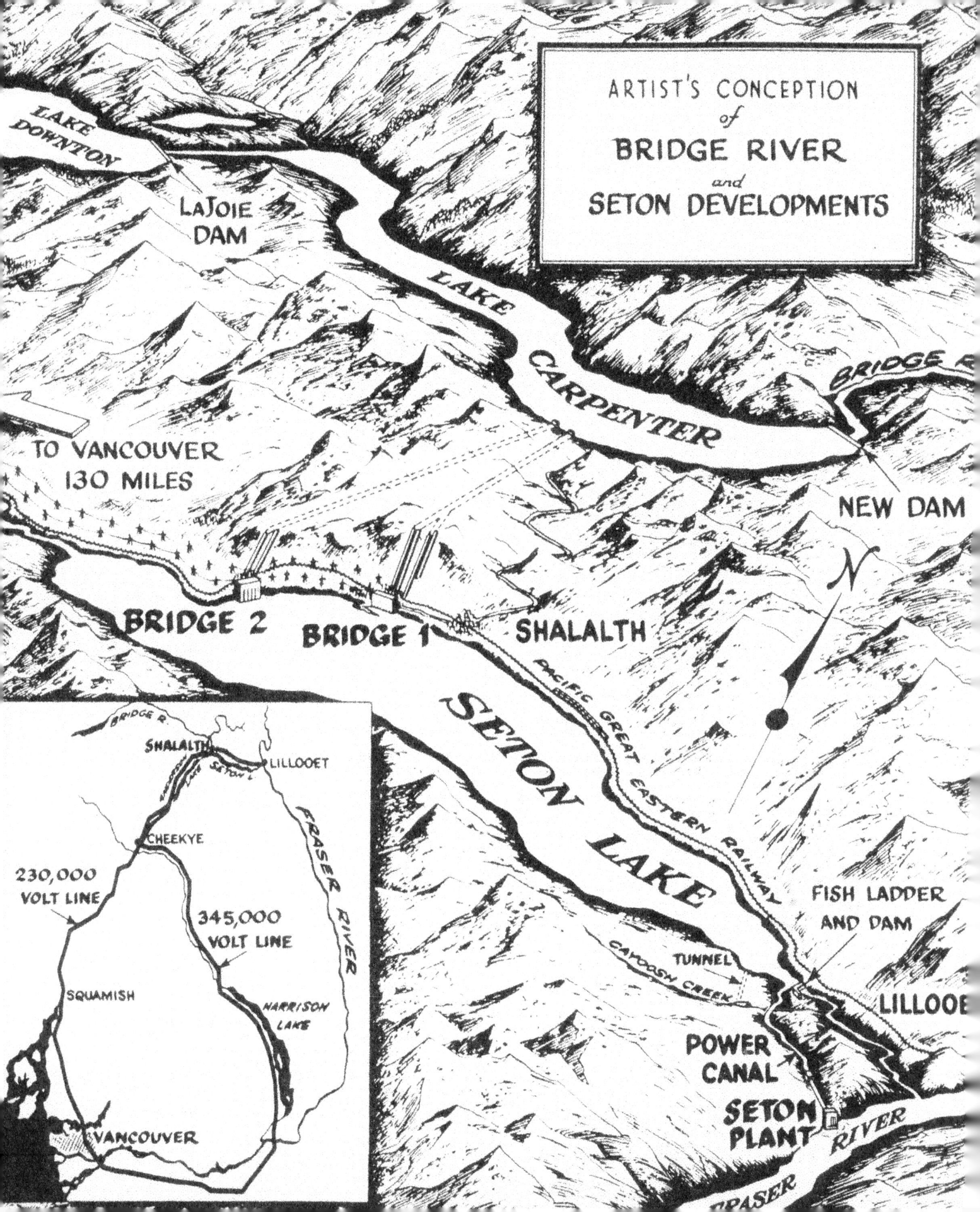

ARTIST'S CONCEPTION of BRIDGE RIVER and SETON DEVELOPMENTS

Introduction

At its heart, this is a book about the people who have passed through and settled down in the majestic Bridge River region of British Columbia's Interior. These people include those who sought to make their fortunes from its abundant resources, those who lived off the land and those who built infrastructure for the broader economic growth of the province. It is also about the people of the St'át'imc Nation, who have lived in the region for thousands of years. In the late eighteenth and early nineteenth centuries came the British explorers Alexander Mackenzie and then Simon Fraser, who made the first contact in the area, keen to exploit its fur-trading potential. A rush of international prospectors followed fifty or so years later, drawn there for its wealth of gold and jade. Canadians of Japanese descent were forced to relocate there during the Second World War, into internment camps. And there were the workers who came in the late nineteenth century and early to mid part of the twentieth century, to teach, to run stores and government offices, to grow orchards and run ranches and farms, to operate canneries, to mine minerals, and to build, at the time, one of the biggest power projects in British Columbia, which would ultimately supply electricity to the rapidly growing Lower Mainland and southern Vancouver Island.

These lives intersected, and as a result Bridge River has come to mean many things to many people. In the most literal sense, it is the 75-mile (121-km) glacier-fed tributary of the massive Fraser River that once snaked through the Bridge River Valley, whose upper reaches teemed with salmon until the Bridge River was dammed in 1948. The river water was diverted through a tunnel in Mission Mountain and through power turbines, then into Seton Lake. The river likely got its name because of the Indigenous-built footbridge that crossed at a narrow point near where the Bridge River meets the Fraser River. French Canadian employees working for the North West Company in Fort Kamloops had named it Rivière du Pont, which translates to Bridge River. Before that, Fraser had called it Shaw's River, after Angus Shaw, one of the directors of the North West Company, which eventually joined the Hudson's Bay Company.

More broadly, Bridge River refers to the valley through which the river twists and turns under a fortress of claustrophobic canyon walls before it widens and flattens out. The St'át'imc called the Bridge River Valley, particularly the location of Carpenter Reservoir, "the valley of plenty" because of the abundance of fish, wildlife, vegetation, plant medicines and minerals.

FACING This early conceptual drawing of the use of the energy of the Bridge River hydraulic system for power production captured the imagination of developers. Courtesy of the Royal BC Museum

This valley of plenty is over 11,000 acres (4,600 hectares) — more than ten times the size of Vancouver's Stanley Park. Since the withdrawal of the Tsilhqot'in (Chilcotin) from the area during the gold rush, the Bridge River Valley has been at the heart of the way of life of the St'át'imc, who felt first-hand the impact of white contact and the newcomers' pursuit of resource-based industries, and the wealth they offered.

The region is uniquely different from the province's west coast, with a variety of geological rock formations, an abundance of ore deposits, and much hotter and drier summers and colder winters. The Bridge River Valley lies between BC's rugged Coast Mountains to the west and the Fraser River to the east. At the top of Mission Mountain, which is 4,000 feet (1,200 metres) high, coastal air meets with the dry arid air of the Lillooet Valley, forming a unique and unpredictable microclimate. The rivers and lakes are fed by glacial meltwater that flows from the Lillooet ice field and the Chilcotin Range to the north where ranchers have raised livestock in wide open meadows since the late nineteenth century. Historic cabins, signs of pioneering homesteaders, still dot the landscape. The region is abundant with the wildlife for which the province is known, including grizzly and black bears, bighorn sheep, mountain goats, cougars, bobcats, lynx, moose, coyotes, deer, beavers, wolverines and hundreds of bird species.

Thousands of years ago, a massive rockslide divided a glacier-fed lake into two lakes, today known as Seton and Anderson Lakes. These are deep lakes, in some places as deep as sea level, at 1,470 feet (450 metres), and were at one time rich with trout, salmon and freshwater lingcod. The water from the lakes empties into a creek at the eastern end of Seton Lake and flows into the Fraser River, where it runs just south of the town of Lillooet. Between the two lakes, the narrow strip of land that formed is called Seton Portage, which is five miles (8 km) from the community of Shalalth, home of the Tsal'alh (formerly the Seton Lake Band).

South Shalalth, which sits at the base of Mission Mountain, is where the first powerhouses were built to generate electricity and transmit it 150 miles (240 km) to Vancouver — an ambitious undertaking that began in the 1920s, after railway surveyors working prior to the First World War first visualized the area's hydroelectric power potential. The entire hydroelectric system was nicknamed "Bridge River," and the two main powerhouses were completed in 1948 and 1960, on the shores of Seton Lake, where a company townsite was also built. There are smaller powerhouses within the system, including one at the headwaters of the Bridge River — Lajoie Dam and powerhouse, finished about 1955 — and the Seton powerhouse on the Fraser River, just downstream of the outflow from Seton Lake, which incorporates a fish ladder and a diversion canal, completed in 1956.

The Bridge River system has had a profound impact on the people of the St'át'imc Nation. Its development altered watersheds and changed ecosystems, and the associated impacts on fish and fish habitat remain a very significant concern to the St'át'imc way of life. For that reason, the experience of the St'át'imc is a big part of this hydro development story.

After the launch of the project's first generation unit (or turbine-generator set) in 1948, it would become the province's biggest hydroelectric project for the next two decades. Upon its completion in 1960, the project was supplying more than half of the electricity needed to power the Lower Mainland. Today, Bridge 1 and Bridge 2 combined provide the Lower Mainland with about 480,000 kilowatts, or about 5 percent of BC Hydro's supply — about enough to power the city of Surrey. It may sound small, but it is substantial, and about half the power that Site C on the Peace River is projected to provide.

Bridge River, or simply "Bridge," is also a reference to the townsite that was built for the workers who constructed, operated and maintained the power plants. For three decades it was a thriving company town filled with families, many of them from foreign countries and starting new lives. But once the Bridge 1 powerhouse was fully automated like Bridge 2, in the 1980s, the company town was significantly reduced in size and the powerhouses operated with a smaller staff, with most employees staying the week and returning home to places like Mission, Abbotsford, Lillooet or Kamloops on the weekends. From then on, the four plants at Bridge River were operated from the control centre on top of Burnaby Mountain. (Today the control centre is located in Langley.)

The genesis of the Bridge River power project goes back more than 100 years, with discussions starting around 1912. In the late 1920s, the plan to harness energy started out with a plan for a 130-mile (210-km) transmission line that would bring power to the Lower Mainland. But due to the Great Depression the plan was downscaled in 1934 to a single temporary generating unit and a 54-mile (87-km) transmission line to service nearby mining operations at Bralorne, in the upper reaches of the Bridge River Valley. After the war, the project became instrumental to servicing a booming population in Vancouver, requiring transmission lines over some of Canada's most rugged terrain. To achieve this, workers bored a pair of two-and-a-half-mile (4-km) tunnels through Mission Mountain, which stood between Bridge River and Seton Lake. The first tunnel, completed in 1931, was used to supply water to a small temporary unit that had been relocated from Jordan River on Vancouver Island to power nearby mines. The second tunnel would be built between 1958 and 1960.

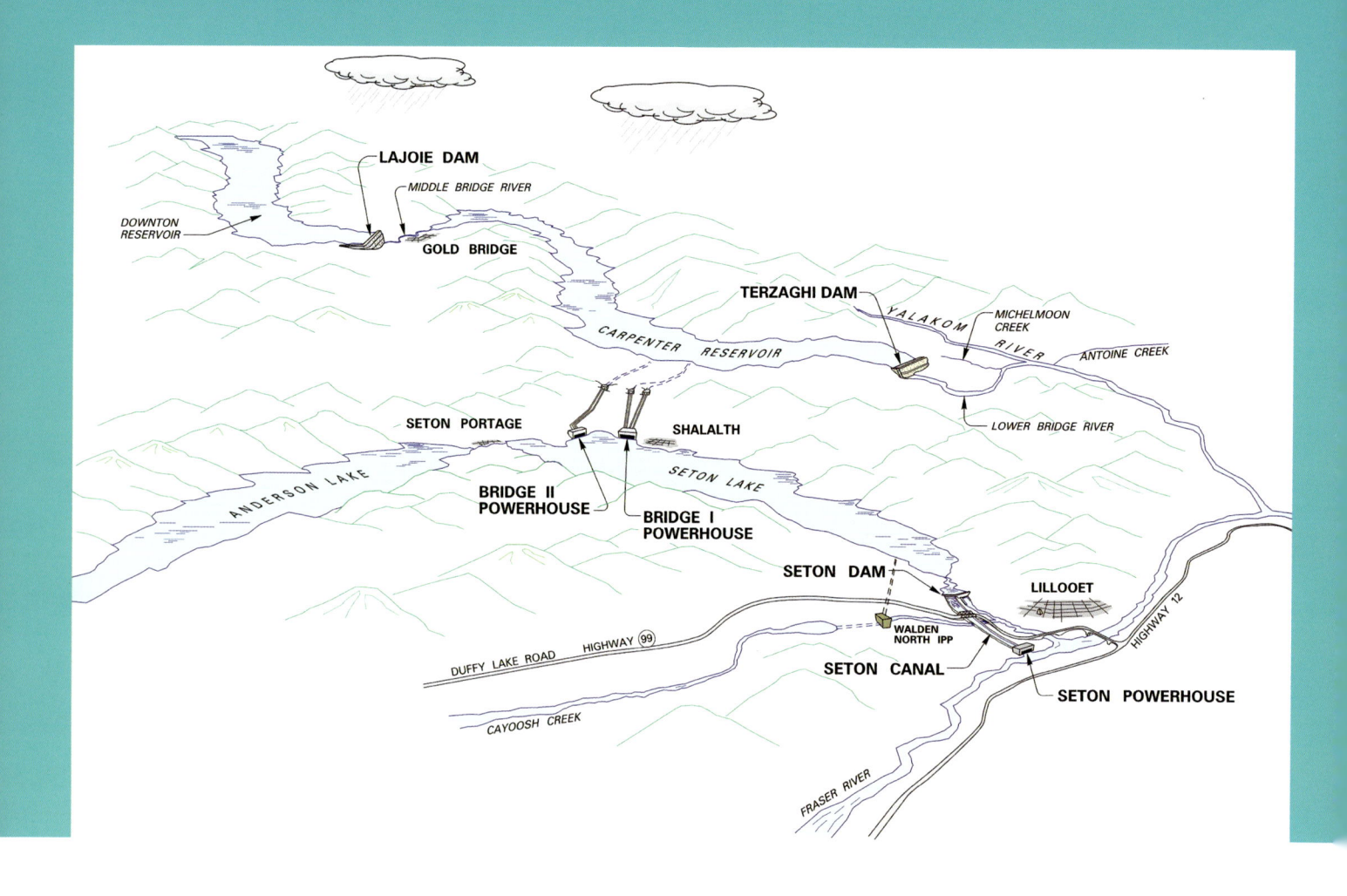

By some odd stroke of nature, the Bridge River was 1,200 feet (370 metres) higher than Seton Lake, so they diverted the river water into the tunnels through Mission Mountain down giant penstocks (pipes) and into turbines, generating electricity before it flowed into Seton Lake. And on the other end of Seton Lake, the water would be used yet again, contained by a small concrete headworks on the Seton River, with a water drop of 50 feet (15 metres). The water would flow through a canal that was 12,500 feet (3,800 metres) long from dam to powerhouse, then spill through the turbine at a smaller single-unit power generation plant before exiting into the Fraser River.

The project was a major employer. From the late 1940s to the early 1960s, thousands of men from around BC who worked in engineering and the construction trades would have worked at Bridge, most full-time, and others during the summer. A few women, too, found jobs as teachers, retail workers and secretaries at the townsite.

VOICES FROM BRIDGE RIVER

The diversion of the river and the flooding of the Bridge River Valley changed the landscape. On the north side of Mission Mountain, where the valley had been, there was a new reservoir: a man-made lake that was named after the BC Electric staff engineer who oversaw the project, E.E. Carpenter. As a result of the Terzaghi Dam (formerly Mission Dam), the Bridge River flow below its location was greatly reduced. The entire undertaking eventually comprised three dams, a lake and two water reservoirs for four generating stations. They built a system that used the water three times to generate 492 megawatts, becoming one of Canada's biggest hydro projects of the era.

However, the harnessing of a major river and the flooding of a beautiful and bountiful valley had impacts on both people and the environment. "You would never get approval now for diverting a river like that, from one watershed to another," says BC Hydro president and CEO Chris O'Riley. "It's just so impactful. It's not something you would do today."

The Carpenter Reservoir that occupies the floor of the valley is 30 miles (50 km) long and a milky green colour because of the glacial sediments it holds. When the river was initially dammed in 1948, it flooded half the valley and the wildlife moved on. Once the dam was constructed to its full height, the valley floor was flooded entirely, inundating the mining town of Minto City. Before the hunters supplying the mines at the upper end of the valley took their toll, the valley of plenty, where Carpenter Reservoir is now, was so full of mule deer that it is said that people would only have to step a few feet outside their doors before spotting one. In addition, the reach of the Bridge River that remained downstream of Terzaghi Dam did not provide the same quantity or quality of habitat for returning salmon, an alteration that threw the salmon stocks off course. The salmon runs had been vital to the St'át'imc way of life for all of its history. Salmon made up more than 60 percent of the people's diet.

Although it was soon eclipsed in magnitude by the Peace and Columbia River hydroelectricity projects of the early 1960s through to the 1980s, Bridge River continues to supply enough electricity to power about 300,000 homes a year. In terms of generation, it ranks eighth among BC Hydro generation operations throughout the province. But for the business and industry class of the time, the project was

FACING Water from the glacier-fed Bridge River would be used three times, falling more than 1,800 feet (550 metres) from Lajoie generating station through the Bridge River powerhouses and finally the Seton powerhouse near Lillooet on the Fraser River. Courtesy of BC Hydro Library and Archives

heralded a state-of-the-art, almost unfathomable achievement of human ingenuity and determination.

The Bridge River undertaking took decades, stalled by the Great Depression and then the Second World War. It embodied the sky-is-the-limit mentality of the industrialists of the late nineteenth and early twentieth centuries, when powerful men from Europe, eastern Canada and the US scoured the province in search of profitable ventures. This was before power became a public utility in the West. A private company called BC Electric Railway (BCER) built Bridge River and only in 1961 did it become part of the public utility known today as BC Hydro, which was incorporated in 1962. While reading this book, take note that BCER (BC Electric Railway) and BCE (BC Electric) are the same company. However, the organization of the company changed in 1946; it was at that point that part of BCER became BCE.

Today British Columbians may take for granted that power is a publicly owned and regulated resource, but in those early decades, citizens looked to private entrepreneurs for their infrastructure — not just to light their homes, but to shuttle them around on streetcars and to keep their washing machines running.

These were the days of powerful cigar-smoking men in their city offices, men in suits who were constantly on the lookout for a profit-making enterprise, and they saw BC as a vast, untapped, highly exploitable resource. Their lives of privilege deeply contrasted those of the workers who did the dirty, hard work of building dams and mining deep inside rock, blasting for gold and other minerals, which often involved tremendous risk. It's difficult to imagine the challenge of descending deep into a mine shaft each day, or climbing a 100-foot (30-metre) tower to construct heavy transmission lines. The BCER contractors erected 699 steel towers by 1948, through mountain terrain, each made out of 10 to 20 tons of galvanized steel. A tower with 230-kilovolt lines has three cables and a tower with 360-kilovolt lines has six cables. The linemen strung up 130 miles (210 km) of these inch-thick cables, weighing nearly 1,100 tons, on slopes as steep as 30 degrees — without the aid of helicopters. A crew stringing up the wires would include around sixty-five men.

Pioneering engineers and surveyors were more like explorers, mapping out regions that had never been extensively mapped before. They undertook the construction of dams and tunnels and roadways through incredibly rough terrain, at a time when instruments were little more than compasses, protractors and plumb bobs, and they used horses for stringing transmission conductors and dynamite for blasting. (After the Second World War, they used bulldozers modified to carry large reels of conductor to string the lines.) They were trailblazers in their fields, discovering and testing new technological advancements for the generations of engineers and builders that would come up behind them. Because they were so in demand in this era of giant capital expenditures, many of them gained reputations throughout North America, becoming wealthy men in their own right.

Bridge River was a full-fledged company town, filled with workers and their families, with housing, a community hall and a tennis court provided for by the company, and a superintendent who acted as mayor of the town. It was one among many company towns that used to exist throughout the province in the mid-twentieth century, built upon ample industry and resource extraction. The families that resettled to these remote places made the growth possible.

The company itself, BC Electric Railway, operated in BC but was run from London, England, until December 1928, and then it was run from Montreal. It embarked on an ambitious program to bring buses, streetcars and interurban railway cars, coal gas and electricity to the urban areas of the province. It built dams and transmission lines that were some of the biggest and most advanced in the world, including the two dams at Bridge River, two of the largest man-made structures in Canada at the time.[1] It was one of the biggest and most important hydroelectric projects in Canada in terms of complexity and size.[2] Bridge River was the last major project for BC Electric, before the provincial government expropriated the company and amalgamated it with the BC Power Commission, in 1961.

To that end, Bridge River marked the end of an era of privately owned power in BC. And it marked the beginning of the postwar economic boom that would overtake the province as it entered a new phase of major growth. The hydro project was the catalyst for this growth, and a key part of the wave of major infrastructure that was undertaken in BC in the second half of the twentieth century. However, it also meant major economic and cultural changes for the St'át'imc, with the Bridge River development impacting the heart of their traditional territory.

Voices from
Bridge River

1

Potential Power

> *"The everlasting search for wealth locked in the ground by Nature has made the Bridge River district famous since its gold rush days of 1896."*
>
> — BCE NEWS —

On a hot summer day in 1912, Geoffrey Downton and Patrick Dick Booth stood on Mission Ridge and looked 4,000 feet (1,200 metres) down at the lake that glistened in the sun below. On horseback, they had made the steep climb up the narrow, twisting dirt wagon road over the mountain. Before that, the road had been a pack trail, widened by gold-seeking prospectors in the decades before. And for millennia before that, the Indigenous people of the region would have worn their own pathways through the rugged territory.

The once remote area was opening up to outsiders, and to economic possibility. The Pacific Great Eastern (PGE) Railway was coming. The rail company had incorporated that same year, with plans to provide a Vancouver to Prince George link. The Squamish to Lillooet section of the line was only three years away. Because of the railway, and its access to a wealth of resources, many believed that Lillooet was destined to be a major city. Downton, a surveyor, map maker and draftsman, and Booth, a surveyor and civil engineer, had been hired by the province to survey the area for the rash of pre-emptions that were underway — land claims by settlers who were seeking to mine for gold or start ranches and farms. In the eyes of these newcomers, this was the Wild West, and surveyors were there to figure out who was claiming what. This was at a time when nobody would have thought to include the First Nation communities scattered throughout the territory, who were represented by the federal government's Indian agents. The settlers making claims needed surveys.

Downton and Booth used mountain peaks to triangulate distance and elevation. What they hadn't known before they made the arduous climb up the mountain — which is more than an hour's drive from Lillooet today — is that the valley from which they had climbed was an astonishing 1,200 feet (370 metres) lower than the Bridge River Valley on the other side of the mountain. That elevation difference meant something to their surveyors' eyes. It meant opportunity, because this was 1912, and British Columbia, rich with untapped resources, was brimming with possibility. The discovery of a water drop like that one was like tapping into a gold vein. Here, in this glistening lake below them, Downton and Booth could see the potential to generate power.

It wasn't an unusual thought for that enterprising pair of men. For the last couple of decades, capitalists had been damming rivers and harnessing the rushing water to generate electric power — and profits — all over the world. The higher the drop of water, the more power generated. Power was at the heart of progress because it enabled manufacturing, mining, processing, industry, commerce, and town and city building. Hydroelectricity was still relatively new as a way to provide that power. In the 1880s, businesses had relied on small, local coal-fired and steam-generated electricity until the advent of high voltage alternating current electrical transmission lines allowed for bigger projects in more remote locations of the province by the 1890s.

The technological advancements had made BC a draw for business opportunists, starting with Trout Lake in 1903 (called Buntzen Lake after 1905). Add to this scenario a population boom in the Lower Mainland, and the search for power was an obvious one — and BC's economy would be built on inexpensive electricity.

Incredibly — because the monumental task and the technology needed to do it were formidable — Downton and Booth envisioned a tunnel that would divert the majority of Bridge River two and a half miles (4 km) through the mountain and come out the other side, 1,200 feet (370 metres) above Seton Lake. The river water would drop into the lake through massive pipes called penstocks — comprising a controlled man-made waterfall — where turbines would capture the energy from the water and turn it into electricity. It would mean hauling supplies from 150 miles (240 km) away. It would mean building an entire townsite, with all the necessary amenities, in order to muster the crew to make it happen. It would mean damming the Bridge River — a tributary of the Fraser River — in order to create a reservoir. It would mean expropriating land and flooding out Indigenous territories, homesteads and ranches, as well as small towns, and transforming the region. All because of Downton and Booth's vision, it would become the biggest hydroelectric project in BC — a testament to the postwar era's state-of-the-art hydraulic technology and the political will to build major infrastructure in the name of a big, bold new era.

Downton and Booth's downtown Vancouver office was in the same building as the engineering offices of W.R. Bonnycastle, a prominent hydroelectric engineer who'd relocated from Virginia in 1909 and had been working around BC. They were also promoters, like an early-days start-up company that would buy the rights to a site with development potential with the idea of selling it to someone with deeper pockets. These engineers and surveyors were highly influential men who worked on major projects and were rewarded handsomely enough that they could afford grand art deco and arts and crafts houses in Vancouver's toniest neighbourhoods, including Shaughnessy and Southwest Marine Drive. The company's offices were in the handsome new Rogers Building at 470 Granville Street, which still stands today, with its granite facade and terra cotta details. The interior had white Italian marble throughout its hallways and staircases, a testament to the celebrated careers of those occupying the offices. The building was named

Captain Patrick Dick Booth, DSO, MC, graduated with high honours in engineering from the University of Edinburgh at the age of twenty. He arrived from Scotland in 1908, and became a surveyor in BC in 1910. Courtesy of the University of Edinburgh

after Jonathan Rogers, a Welshman who came to Vancouver as a teenager and went on to become a prominent builder, responsible for many of the buildings along Granville Street.

Many expert engineers had come to BC from around the world, having worked in California or as far afield as the Congo. The engineers and surveyors of the time, says University of British Columbia geography professor Matthew Evenden, "were a diverse group with connections around the world."[1] Downton, from Norfolk, England, was a draftsman who became a surveyor in 1912. A journalist once described him as having the manner of a "retired professor" or "Anglican parson."[2] Booth had begun his civil engineering studies at the University of Edinburgh with the prestigious Arthur Trevelyan engineering scholarship in 1906. Only two such scholarships were given out each year, at an amount of 17 pounds per annum, for proficiency in engineering "and the mechanical and useful arts." He arrived from Scotland in 1908 and became a surveyor in BC in 1910. He was only twenty-six years old in 1912 when he and Downton formed Booth & Downton, a firm that mostly focused on land surveying. They were part of a group that included engineer Bonnycastle, and they incorporated the Bridge River Power Company on December 5, 1912. Downton and Booth became directors.

Downton, as resident agent, applied for the water rights to the Bridge River, and the rights to build a tunnel through Mission Mountain for "irrigation and power purpose." They applied to "make, build, construct, erect, lay down, and maintain reservoirs, waterworks, cisterns, dams, canals, tunnels, culverts, flumes, conduits, pipes, and appliances..." for the creation and development of hydraulic, electrical or mechanical power to be used for any purpose.[3] The licence gave the company the right to use 1,500 cubic feet (42 cubic metres) per second of water out of the Bridge River, "which flows in an easterly direction through Lillooet District and empties into the Fraser River five miles north of the town of Lillooet," it was announced in the publication where such filings were made, the *British Columbia Gazette*, on January 2, 1913.

They acquired funding from capitalist Jonathan Rogers, J. Fyfe Smith, a hardwood products dealer, financier John Williams and lawyer Adolphus Williams, who joined the Bridge

River Power Company in 1913. They established their head office in architect Thomas Mawson's offices in the Rogers Block. The land would be used for power development purposes, said their application, which also mentioned that it would be "on the land described as Seton Lake Indian Reserve, No. 1."[4] Notices were posted in the *British Columbia Gazette* as well as at the diversion site and the powerhouse site.[5]

Downton and Booth returned to Bridge River with a survey crew, to make the first proper surveys, including the proposed locations of future reservoirs. This time they were under the direction of engineer Bonnycastle, who had taken charge of the project and had his own stake in it. They surveyed the location for the reservoir, at the lower part of the river, and worked their way across Mission Mountain, determining the tunnel length, as well as the future powerhouse site to the south. When they were done, they filed their surveys in Victoria, estimating that the project would be completed in five years, which proved to be an overly ambitious goal. The outbreak of the First World War in 1914 curtailed their plans. Downton joined the Canadian Army in 1915 and Booth joined the British Army, since he'd already been in service while attending the University of Edinburgh. Both Downton and Booth were shipped off to France, and both were made captains and awarded military crosses. Downton made it home. Booth died of battle wounds near Les Rues Vertes, on December 1, 1917.

The fledgling company's lofty plan to develop Bridge River began to flounder, for a few reasons. Bridge River Power was in a vulnerable position in this early period, largely because a major power supply wasn't yet in demand. The war effort was also consuming all available capital — they lacked funds. In November 1916, on behalf of the company, Bonnycastle offered the City of Vancouver a three-month option to purchase their claim for the price of $40,000.[6] The city council rejected the offer, likely because they couldn't afford the $5 million required to develop it. Also, Bridge River was a remote region, and a huge endeavour compared to other sites much closer to the urban core. The claim to water rights on the Bridge River was to expire in 1917, but because of Booth's and Downton's war service, the government gave the Bridge River Power Company an extension to March 22, 1920. Booth and Downton had been paid $2,000 each for their discovery of the site and for their survey work. Considering that the average wage at the time was about $2,200 a year, they were handsomely rewarded. Bonnycastle stayed on at the company as a hired engineer. Downton came on as an employee as well, and the water rights were eventually extended again, to April 1, 1926. The extension was a lifeline, because water rights were expensive, and became a key part of the deal for the Montreal syndicate that would purchase Bridge River Power in 1920.

The BC Electric Railway (BCER) syndicate made a play to purchase the Bridge River Power

Company, but the Montreal syndicate beat them to it. Unlike the British Empire Trust, which owned BCER, the Montreal syndicate was looking to make a short-term investment and quick money. Wheelers and dealers looking for quick opportunities dominated these early days of western Canadian industry. Most of the entrepreneurs were based in eastern Canada, the economic hub of the country. And they had powerful connections, with overlapping interests in various businesses.

The Montreal group was made up of a number of eastern players. In 1920, John R. Read, engineer and salesman for Westinghouse, had joined forces with Westinghouse president N.S. Braden, as part of a consortium. Westinghouse was a gigantic American electrical manufacturing company, founded in Pittsburgh in 1886. It had iconic roots. Early on, it rivalled Thomas Edison's company, and its most famous engineer was Nikola Tesla, the inventor who played a key role in designing alternating current (AC) supply. His technology made possible low to high voltage transformation, and the transmission of power over long distances, unlike Edison's direct current (DC) generation technology. The company had a presence in Canada with a manufacturing plant in Hamilton, Ontario. The group also included railway entrepreneur H.T. Vaughn, who had started with Canadian Pacific Railway and became part of the famous Canadian Northern Railway railway-building empire founded by Sir William Mackenzie and Sir Donald Mann.

The biggest shareholder of the new company was the major Montreal stock brokerage Royal Securities Corporation, which held almost half of the issued share capital. Royal Securities had handled the financing for another BC project, the Stave Lake Power Company, and it had financed Calgary Power. Under Izaak Walton Killam, Royal Securities became one of Canada's largest brokerages.

To put the status of these men in perspective, Killam would be considered Canada's wealthiest man by the time of his death in 1955. It made sense that the company would be interested in Bridge River Power, because Killam had moved aggressively into financing the pulp and paper industry, which required the electrical generating stations to power their operations. Royal Securities had once been run by Arthur Nesbitt, who would go on to become co-founder of Nesbitt, Thomson & Company, the company behind the Power Corporation of Canada. However, Nesbitt and the Power Corporation of Canada weren't involved in Bridge River — not yet. At this point, the Montreal syndicate of shareholders was only a precursor to the giant Power Corporation of Canada, the power empire that would, in a few years' time, play a key role in Bridge River. For now, though, the eastern businessmen were more interested in flipping their new asset for a profit, and that profit was to be found in London, with the BC Electric Railway Company (BCER), which had already been conducting feasibility studies on the power potential of the site. The easterners would have been well aware of these studies.

The Scoundrel Joseph Lajoie

There is perhaps no better story to illustrate the Wild West recklessness of the BC Interior in the early part of the twentieth century than that of Joseph Zotique Lajoie. Lajoie, also nicknamed Lazack Lajoie, made a lot of claims, some of which were true, some of which weren't. A magazine article from 1914 touted Lajoie as "a pioneer of the Bridge River country" because of his relentless boosterism of its resources.[7]

The French Canadian goes down in history as a master in self-promotion who sold a lot of unfortunate people on the idea that the Gun Lake area, just north of the eastern end of what would become the Downton Lake Reservoir, was rich in gold, and a fitting site for a future city. He was frequently called a "huckster."

Lajoie staked eight claims for gold and other minerals in May 1913, at the north end of Gun Lake. He also published a notice of application to buy Crown land in August of that year, as the first step in the founding of the Lajoie townsite. He made seven more claims around what became Lajoie Falls, which he promoted as a rich source of pitchblende, or uranium ore. He signed up twelve clients to a Memorandum of Association, issued ten shares to each of the men, and made them directors of the J.Z. Lajoie Company Limited. Lajoie received 575,010 shares as payment for the deal.

He proposed that his townsite wouldn't be a boomtown, but rather a naturally expanding place that would grow to 5,000 people in a five-year span. He claimed to have found a vein of ore at Lajoie Falls that was 12 feet (3.5 metres) wide. However, Lajoie hadn't made proper application for acquiring Crown land, so there was no townsite. By June 11, 1914, all of the mining claims had lapsed.

Lajoie also said he'd made a water claim, with a promise to produce 150,000 horsepower at Lajoie Falls. That particular claim was surprisingly prophetic, considering it would eventually become the site of a powerhouse. However, the Water Act of BC was rewritten in 1914 and did not allow anyone to stake a waterpower site that required a large amount of money for development. The idea was to discourage people from speculating on potential waterpower sites, holding onto them and demanding a lot of money once power development companies came calling.

But the facts would have been unknown to the twenty or so men who were sent to the Lajoie Falls campsite in the summer of 1914 to construct the townsite. A post office was erected and bunkhouses were on the way. However, the men were paid in shares, and by spring, they were going to revolt if they didn't see a paycheque. Lajoie, who had a cabin in the townsite, went to his Vancouver headquarters to bring back money — he should have had considerable funds available, since he'd sold more than 55,000 shares and didn't actually hold any assets. But Lajoie disappeared, never to be seen again.

By May 16, 1916, the post office in Lajoie closed and the company went into liquidation. His victims left the townsite, having been hoodwinked, and most went south to Vancouver. Some stayed in the valley and worked as prospectors and trappers, and a couple of the men went off to fight in the First World War. By 1928, gold was mined along the Bridge River, although not at the sites staked by Lajoie — but it was in greater quantities than he'd promised, so he was almost right. As for the water rights he claimed to hold, BC Electric Railway obtained them for the Bridge River power project.

Today, Lajoie Dam and a small powerhouse are situated on top of the Lajoie Falls, forming the Downton Lake Reservoir. Lajoie Lake is a small private lake, better known these days as Little Gun Lake, and drains into Lajoie Creek. And the waterpower Lajoie promised isn't quite as great as he'd envisioned. Instead of 150,000 horsepower, the Lajoie powerhouse generates 22 megawatts, or close to 30,000 horsepower. But the Lajoie Dam serves the crucial purpose of controlling Carpenter Reservoir water levels and the flow of water to the big powerhouses at Seton Lake. His namesake dam contributed to the hydroelectric system that provided more than half the electricity requirements for the Lower Mainland by the time it was completed.

The BC Electric Railway Company

The BCER was formed in 1897, by a group of British investors who had experience in urban transit and very deep pockets. Two of those investors, Robert Montgomery Horne-Payne and Frank Stillman Barnard, proved key players in the early development of BC's hydroelectric power. Barnard, who was born in Toronto and raised in Victoria, was a pioneering businessman with interests in transportation, banking, mining, forestry and real estate. He sat on several boards, including that of the Hastings Sawmill Company, and he ultimately received a knighthood for his service to the country as Lieutenant-Governor of BC. He was behind a company that had purchased several failing transit and light companies in the urban cores of the Lower Mainland at the time, which were Vancouver, New Westminster and the area now known as North Vancouver. That company, the Consolidated Railway and Light Company, had incorporated in 1894 with $1 million in capital provided by local businessmen.

Barnard was aware of the potential of hydroelectric power because of his involvement in various industrial pursuits. But it wasn't until he met Horne-Payne that he fully saw the financial potential of hydroelectricity. As the story goes, Barnard made a journey to Nelson, when he was travelling on business as director of the Columbia and Kootenay Navigation Company, that was to have far-reaching consequences. While there, taking a ride on the deck of a small steamer on Kootenay Lake, he met British entrepreneur Horne-Payne, who had great ambitions for the new frontier of western Canada. The young Horne-Payne had come to Canada as a partner in Sperling and Company, one of London's most prestigious stockbrokerages, and he was in Nelson to meet the president of the Canadian Pacific Railway. He'd been invited on a long journey to inspect the entire CPR from the Atlantic to the Pacific, which had given him the steely determination to sink an unprecedented $500 million worth of British capital into Canadian industry (which he would do by the time of his death in 1929). Barnard invited him and Sir William Van Horne, the CPR president, to tour mining developments underway around Kootenay Lake.

Horne-Payne would go on to become a railway tycoon, providing the backing for the Canadian Northern Railway and sitting as its London director a few years later. But the financier would oversee mining, oil, coal and other interests in BC as well. He was always on the lookout for an opportunity, as long as he could make his 5 percent, at minimum. It was while on this short Kootenay tour that Horne-Payne realized the tremendous development potential of light and power. Horne-Payne was enthusiastic, and by the time he met with Barnard, who he deemed a worthy partner, he was keen to do business.[8]

Horne-Payne returned to England and secured funding to pay off Consolidated Railway and Light Company's debts as well as funding for future growth. He came back to BC and rejoined Barnard to purchase the Victoria Electric Railway and Lighting Company. However, their ambitious new plans were thwarted by tragedy on May 24, 1896, when a Victoria streetcar overly packed with 140 people for Victoria Day celebrations fell into Rock Bay when the bridge under it collapsed. Horne-Payne and Barnard hadn't been able to board the crowded streetcar, and had gone on ahead on foot.

When they heard the crushing sound of the bridge collapsing, they ran back and helped rescue anyone they could. But fifty-five people died that day, and news of the disaster travelled to London. Fearing the scandal of liability, the syndicate that had promised their funding withdrew the money. The public and the press held Horne-Payne and Barnard's company accountable for the disaster, and lawsuits were filed. With so much legal liability, they lost control of the company to bondholders. In the end, an investigation showed that the collapse was due to faulty bridge structure, and not the streetcar system. But almost a year had passed, and Horne-Payne had returned to London. When the company was cleared of wrongdoing, he again scrabbled together the necessary capital and returned to BC to start over again.

Robert Montgomery Horne-Payne. Courtesy of the Royal BC Museum

Barnard and Horne-Payne then registered a new company in London, on April 3, 1897, called the British Columbia Electric Railway Company Limited, better known simply as BCER. Their goal was to run their railway system on water-powered electricity as opposed to thermal, which had been costly. Thermal electricity was cheap to build, but expensive to run. Hydroelectricity was expensive to build, but cheap to run. To do that, they sought to develop their own hydroelectric power sources, starting with a dam at Buntzen Lake in 1903. The enterprising duo would go on to develop one of the most extensive electric railway systems in the world. As Cecil Maiden wrote in *Lighted Journey*, his history of BC Electric, thanks to Barnard and Horne-Payne, "B.C. Electric had stepped upon the stage of Canadian history." [9]

With Barnard serving as the managing director, the company directors held their first meeting on April 15, 1897. They incorporated the Vancouver Power Company on January 20, 1898, as a subsidiary. They hadn't noticed there was a provision in the Water Clauses Consolidation Act of 1897 that limited them to generating electricity by thermal means. But instead of waiting for the legislation to change, they formed the Vancouver Power Company so they could go ahead and stake water rights.

Barnard made an unfortunate decision when he spent $25,000 on a streetcar line in Victoria just before the economy went down. He quickly lost favour with the London office. Barnard's position was therefore brief; he resigned as managing director and sat as a board member instead. Johannes Buntzen, who'd arrived in Vancouver in the 1890s from Copenhagen, replaced him. Buntzen was a visionary who realized that the company needed to act fast because it was facing significant competition — most notably from the Stave Lake Power Company, whose board members included John Hendry and Sir Charles Hibbert Tupper, son of former prime minister Sir Charles Tupper.

BCER's head office was in London, with Horne-Payne in charge, and their Canadian headquarters was in downtown Vancouver. With the depression of 1893 to 1897 over, demand was on again for streetcars, and with municipal approval, the system expanded in New Westminster, Vancouver and Victoria, where populations were booming. A lot of growth occurred in the early twentieth century, with streetcar lines built out to North Vancouver and interurban lines to Chilliwack, and work starting on a major hydroelectric project at Jordan River, on Vancouver Island, as well as ongoing work on the Buntzen power plant.

BCER increased its coal gas manufacturing division and built a big new headquarters at Carrall and Hastings. In 1907, George Kidd responded to a London newspaper ad for a job with the company, and four years later he left the London office to work as comptroller in the Vancouver office. By 1914, he was general manager. The year before, another English national arrived, William George Murrin, and he was appointed general superintendent in charge of the city and suburban transportation departments.

An ongoing concern for BCER at the time was the possibility that the City of Vancouver would take them over. In 1901, the city had an agreement with the BCER that gave it the option to purchase the company's electricity and transportation holdings within the city after 1919, and every five years from then on. That agreement would haunt the British syndicate, which is why the BCER would attempt to purchase utilities and transportation rights all around the city of Vancouver. They were poised for competition, and by owning the other transit lines outside the Vancouver boundary, they were making it logistically impossible for the city to do a takeover. Fortunately for the company, the city would never have the funds to compete.

The Bridge River Power Company had been entertaining all sorts of schemes since it incorporated, including a proposal by an American company that wanted to manufacture nitrogen fertilizer for explosives during the First World War. That same company, American Nitrogen, had an operation at the Buntzen power plant manufacturing nitric acid, which was a compound in trinitrotoluene, better known as the explosive TNT. The plan was that postwar, the fertilizers could be shipped to the Prairies by railcar. Big American pulp and paper mills had their sights on Bridge River for power production. And then there were plans for an enormous agricultural facility, which would have needed irrigation. However, none of the plans were realized.

FACING The collapse of the Rock Bay bridge in Victoria on May 24, 1896, almost ended the business interests of Horne-Payne and Barnard in the Victoria Electric Railway and Lighting Company. Courtesy of the Royal BC Museum

The only plan that made sense was for the province's biggest power and transit company, BCER, to take over, and its president, George Kidd, was keen to do so. In 1923, the company obtained an option on the site, which meant they'd purchased the right to buy it by an agreed-upon deadline. It conducted exhaustive studies with the help of Bonnycastle, who sent survey parties to cover the huge territory. A San Francisco engineer named J.D. Galloway was also hired in 1925, and he informed BCER that 700,000 horsepower could be developed at Bridge River—enough power to serve approximately 250,000 homes. BCER's consulting engineer, E.E. Carpenter, who'd worked on the company's Jordan River hydroelectricity project on Vancouver Island, was also hired to work on preliminary study of Bridge River.

To BCER, the Bridge River development was crucial because of positioning in the region by rivals, who were also looking at hydroelectricity opportunities. The large power development at Stave Lake, owned by what was now the Western Canada Power Company, was a serious threat. And Stone & Webster, a formidable engineering and utilities company from Massachusetts, was showing interest in developments in the area. The company had already purchased the Nooksack Falls hydroelectricity plant in nearby Bellingham and wanted to expand northward.

Their primary business rival had evolved over the past two decades. The Stave Lake Company originally had majority shareholder John Hendry at the helm. On July 1, 1909, the Montreal syndicate of Charles H. Cahan, the Bank of Montreal and Royal Securities Corporation, as well as shareholder Charles Hibbert Tupper, purchased the company. They renamed it the Western Canada Power Company, and became BCER's biggest competition. The two companies would go on to have a long and complicated rivalry over Stave Lake, which provided power to more than 1,000 customers by 1913. Bonnycastle had designed the intake dam and the first phase of construction at Stave.

With chairman Horne-Payne guiding from London, and general manager R.H. Sperling in BC (from 1905 to 1914), BCER kept a close watch on Stave Lake Power's financial struggles and the goings-on of the new Montreal syndicate behind the Western Canada Power Company. There were attempted negotiations and business dealings throughout the early part of the twentieth century, prior to the First World War. Some of the conflicts arose regarding the creation of an interurban railway system into Vancouver, which would have threatened BCER's interurban interests. Part of BCER's intense involvement with Stave Lake was also the continued interest of Stone & Webster, who were hovering around the development, looking for an opportunity.

BCER had an agreement signed in 1913 to purchase power from the Western Canada Power Company (WCPC) as it needed it. WCPC also had an agreement to supply Bellingham across the border with power, so it had moved into the US market. The company focused on supplying industry with power, and it needed the customers. Although financially hobbled, WCPC managed to install Generating Unit No. 3 at Stave Falls in 1916, but Unit No. 4 was delayed due to the war. At this time, the company restructured itself and became the Western Power Company of Canada (WPCC). The company continued to struggle, but BCER's electrical superintendent, J.I. Newell, still saw the company as a serious threat once the economy inevitably rebounded.

Once the war was over, the economy did just that. Suddenly business was booming. A BCER engineer estimated that the company would face a 10 percent annual increase in total electrical load, requiring twice the output in seven to eight years.[10] The company would need to invest $25 million in new projects and transmission lines. BCER needed to expand its hydroelectricity operations quickly, to meet the new demand, so it purchased the financially struggling WPCC in 1920 and built the fourth generating unit.[11] The Stave Lake plant, the biggest electricity-generating facility in western Canada and a technological marvel at the time, became a huge source of pride for the BCER.

The BCER made plans for another plant downriver at the Ruskin site, to be built in a few years. The original engineers at Stave had identified the perfect location for a plant (Ruskin) that would reuse the same river water and offer a potential 100,000 horsepower that could supply Vancouver, and was only 35 miles (55 km) away. In 1929, construction began on Ruskin Dam and powerhouse at the narrow granite gorge three and a half miles (5.6 km) downstream of Stave Falls, and the project was completed with two generators in 1938. This development created Hayward Lake Reservoir, named after Stave Falls Dam's first production superintendent. Along with the purchase, BCER inherited the water rights. And because the company already owned the water rights to nearby Alouette Lake, they had another option before them: to dam and divert water from the lake through a tunnel to Stave Lake, with a powerhouse on the Stave shore that would generate 12,500 horsepower. The extra water diverted into Stave Lake would also mean the possibility of a fifth unit at Stave Falls. Stave Falls was joining part of an expanding system.

BCER began work on the Alouette project in 1924, starting with tunnelling and a rail spur to the work site. That same year, E.E. Carpenter, the construction engineer for the company, began the feasibility study to determine whether the Bridge River project was an economically sound one. He oversaw a party of fifty engineers who traversed 55 miles (90 km) of the Bridge River Valley, entering into snowfields and glaciers above Lajoie Falls, areas that were pretty much unknown to outsiders. Bridge River sat deep within a canyon, amid mountainous terrain for much of its journey from the snowfields to the Fraser River. Once Carpenter's comprehensive investigation was complete, it was clear that the company was dealing with a major source of hydroelectric power. As Cecil Maiden wrote in *Lighted Journey*, "As the results of the survey began to be tabulated, it was realized that here indeed lay the future main heart and centre of British Columbia's power supply."[12]

But before expansion of its network could happen, BCER would need to pay off the Montreal syndicate — which it did, to the tune of $500,000. Bridge River Power was now entering the era of ownership under British-controlled BCER, which remained a conservatively run company with a keen interest in developing BC's hydroelectric potential.

By September 1925, BCER had purchased the Bridge River Power Company, including its rights and properties, through the purchase of the original company's stock. The acquisition was announced in the *Vancouver Daily Province* newspaper on September 18, 1925. The company, it was reported, would spend $30 million and employ 2,000 men, building one of the continent's largest "water powers," or hydroelectric power plants.

BCER's purchase of Bridge River Power included the development rights to Bridge River. So with the confidence of the engineers' reports, BCER president George Kidd announced at the opening of the fifth generation unit at Stave Falls power plant on September 19, 1925, that the BCER would develop Bridge River.

The BCER was by now a formidable organization, controlling almost all the gas companies and power production plants servicing the Lower Mainland and southern Vancouver Island, including the tiny Goldstream plant, which was the first built by the company, and the first hydroelectricity facility for Victoria, in 1898.

The BCER employed 3,240 staff by the end of June 1926, serving a total population of more than 375,000. Alouette Lake was diverted by tunnel to Stave Lake in 1926, and two years later, the Alouette powerhouse became one of the earliest examples of automation in the Commonwealth. Bridge River would eclipse Ruskin and become BCER's biggest and most complex power development yet, utilizing state-of-the-art technology.[13]

Bridge River had its obstacles, however. Montreal electrical engineer Raymond S. Kelsch had earned his reputation designing some of

Canada's earliest hydroelectric projects in Quebec. Kelsch had so much respect throughout North America that if he thought a project was worthwhile it invariably went ahead. BCER of course consulted with Kelsch, who saw the tremendous potential of Bridge River. But it wasn't lost on him that they would be building a substantial, earth-filled dam in a gorge on a bed of gravel and silt. The powerhouse would also be sitting on an unstable bed of silt, on the shore of Seton Lake. There was also the challenge of

"Here are the men in whose hands the success of the Bridge river project rests. The men are pictured around the testing machine, which is mentioned in the article by Mr. Blee. Left to right in the picture are: W.R. Bonnycastle, engineer in charge; H. Irvine, resident engineer; E. Rexworthy, boatman; E.E. Carpenter, civil engineer; Eric Lazenby, levelman; J.D. Galloway, consulting engineer, and C.E. Blee, assistant engineer." *B.C. Electric Employees' Magazine*, October 1926. Courtesy of BC Hydro Library and Archives

ABOVE One of the initial development concepts was for a tunnel through Mission Mountain and a powerhouse on the shore of Seton Lake. Courtesy of the Royal BC Museum

FACING This sectional view shows one of a number of design concepts of dams and tunnels that would provide the "head" for a powerhouse on Seton Lake. Courtesy of the Royal BC Museum

building 150 miles (240 km) of transmission lines over a heavily timbered, mountainous region. Still, Kelsch was a supporter. In a letter to BCER president Kidd in June 1922, Kelsch had written: "With my 40 years experience in steam and hydro-electric power work, I do not hesitate to say I believe the Bridge River power scheme is possible of being developed and delivering several hundred thousand HP [horsepower] to Vancouver."

With the support of engineers who were giants in their field, George Kidd made Bridge River his mission. Bridge River, he boasted, was considered a record-setting power source, three times higher than Niagara Falls. Every cubic foot of water dropping 1,200 feet (370 metres) would generate 80 kilowatts of electricity.

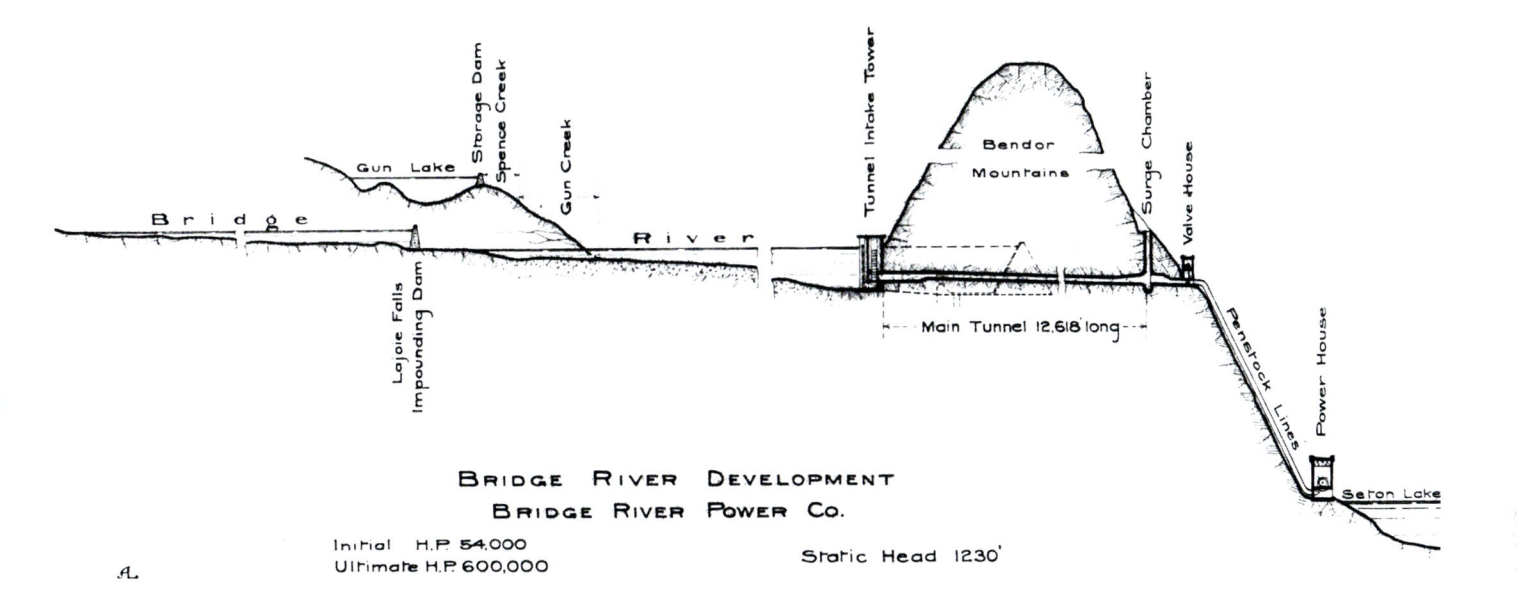

BRIDGE RIVER DEVELOPMENT
BRIDGE RIVER POWER CO.

Initial H.P. 54,000
Ultimate H.P. 600,000
Static Head 1230'

The first stage of planned development — with the installation of two 25,000-horsepower generators — was estimated at a cost of $13,271,000, in a 1925 report prepared for BCER by well-known San Francisco engineer J.D. Galloway.

In an early BCER booklet called *The Bridge River Power Development*, Kidd affirmed the need for big, bold action to sustain the growth of a new city for at least twenty years down the road, as opposed to the constant construction of little projects everywhere. His words also underscore the company's understanding that it needed to be seen as responding to the public's demands. Public relations would have been an important factor for the BCER, especially considering the high rates they were charging residential consumers.

Costly as this development is, the British Columbia Electric Railway company has chosen it because it solves for a score of years or more any problem as to the future supply of power. There are several small potential power developments in the vicinity of Vancouver but with the industrial expansion of the city that is anticipated, the development of any of them would mean an ever-recurring problem of new projects. In this modern age, there must be no question as to the adequacy of electric power supply and as the company serving this territory, the B.C. Electric will not betray its trust to maintain this supply ever in advance of the community's needs.[14]

2

Construction Begins

In order to build the powerhouse, penstocks and transmission lines for the ambitious Bridge River project, the BCER needed to build a townsite of considerable size that would sustain the crew for an estimated twenty to twenty-five years.[1] The townsite would ultimately vary in population size, demographic and purpose, but it would endure.

Work started in 1926 with the building of a 20-foot (6-metre) wide motor vehicle road over Mission Mountain, connecting the Bridge River Valley with the powerhouse site on Seton Lake. The road climbed a summit about 3,000 feet (900 metres) above lake level, with a grade as steep as 16 percent (a 16-foot rise for every 100 feet) in some spots. There are about three dozen sharp turns on the gravel road, and at least a dozen of them are unforgiving hairpin curves with sheer drops. If a truck travelled too fast and lost control, skidding across loose rock, it could be instant tragedy — and it happened many times. But the Caterpillar-like Linn tractors of the day hauled 15-ton loads over the road with ease.

The road construction doubled the seven-foot (2-metre) width of the existing road in order to be able to bring in tons of materials and equipment to build the tunnel and dam. The road would later continue two miles (3 km) downriver, to the main storage and diversion dam for the first plant, nicknamed Bridge 1. In June 1926, a steam shovel was brought in and clearing began for the Bridge River townsite. The PGE Railway had built a large freight yard for equipment, with a hilly area cleared to make way for a passing track and two unloading tracks, plus another one for unloading diesel fuel.

The first contract, dated May 11, 1926, went to two young Indigenous men from Shalalth, according to Cecil Maiden. The men were Patrick Oleman and John Tom, who were hired to cut and place railway ties to support the new tracks. The contract to build a guesthouse, worker cottages, rows of family houses, a hospital, workshops, a community hall, a store, a schoolhouse, offices and bunkhouses with showers went to Vancouver builder S.M. McLeod. A sewer system was installed, as were a domestic water system and fire services. Power was generated by an 1,800-horsepower diesel electric power plant, for the construction and the community. So the workers could set up accounts, the Canadian Imperial Bank of Commerce opened a small branch — a little wooden shack — at the community site in October 1927.

Like everything about the project, the tunnel was a massive undertaking for the time. It was certainly the biggest for the company, at a length of 13,200 feet (4,000 metres). Before completion, its interior walls would be lined with concrete. At Seton Lake, the water inside penstocks would drop 1,200 feet (370 metres) to the power generators at the lakeside, at a grade of about 60 percent. The head, or drop, would be three times greater than Buntzen's and ten times that of Stave Lake. In order to understand the rock that they'd need to bore into, a tiny core sample 1,000 feet (300 metres) in length was taken from the mountain using diamond drills. Early in 1927, the contract for the tunnel went to the same company that built the road, Pacific Engineering. The budget was $2 million, just for the tunnel.[2]

This investigative work was being done at the same time as preliminary groundwork on the dam that would divert the water from Bridge River. Crews spent the summer drilling into the Bridge River bed with diamond drills, trying to find a suitable location for the dam. They went up and down the river boring holes into anything that looked solid, drilling at least three dozen holes up to 200 feet (60 metres) deep. They finally settled on a site about two miles (3 km) downstream of the entrance to the tunnel. The first small dam was to be a temporary 40-foot (12-metre) high "timber crib" structure, an old-fashioned style of temporary dam constructed out of heavy timber and filled with earth or rubble. Small dams would be constructed to divert the water so the crews could work on the permanent dam.

And then the tunnel work began. The engineers had the recent experience of building a half-mile (1-km) tunnel between Alouette and Stave Lakes between 1924 and 1926, so they had the know-how. Colonel W.W. Foster, who'd been highly decorated in the First World War, ran Pacific Engineering and oversaw the tunnel work with military precision. Prior to the war, Colonel Foster had been chief engineer for the City of Vancouver, and had worked on the Canadian Pacific Railway. A hands-on engineer, he had a wealth of experience and was a natural for the job. He had his work cut out for him, too, because the mountain rock was fractured, and draining water into a subterranean lake. Workers were forever battling the drainage, and continue to do so to this day. In tunnel work, drainage issues are part of the job.

One of the survey crew in 1926 was mathematics student Walt Gage, who'd go on to become a celebrated president of the University of British Columbia (UBC), serving from 1969 to 1975. His father A.W.G. Gage, who was a purchasing agent for the BCER, got him the job helping survey the tunnel. It was a good practice in precision for the mathematician. And most of the future engineers who would work on the Bridge River project studied under Gage, who taught engineering mathematics at UBC.

Before the blasting of the tunnel got started, portals for each end of the tunnel were surveyed and the direction of the tunnel determined. This would have taken several days and big crews, working to triangulate the location of the tunnel using nearby mountains. Actual boring through the tunnel was dirty, dangerous, tedious work. Men weren't required to wear hard hats, however. There was no safety officer, and the man in charge of first aid did the best he could. The miners would drill into the rock, pack it with dynamite and blast it out. They used heavy drills that were operated by compressed air to cut a pattern of holes into the rock. Once drilling was completed, they loaded the holes with waxpaper–wrapped dynamite sticks that they would tamp into place with a wood stick. They'd attach a detonator to the end of each stick, and a length of fuse cord to that. The fuse would burn at one foot (30 cm) every 40 seconds.[3] The miners would light the fuse cords and everyone would stand back and count the number of explosions to safeguard against any misfires.

The "muckers" would clear out the rubble, to be followed by the blasting work of the miners again. An engineer would occasionally stop work and take measurements to set the correct alignment and grade of the tunnel. If the work was anything like the Buntzen tunnel experience under Barnard and Horne-Payne's Vancouver Power Company, the miners and muckers were on contract and working in eight-hour shifts, around the clock, seven days a week — and didn't get paid for standing around. If the engineer took too long, they'd get irritated. "They were not averse to throwing rocks at him to hurry up the process," wrote retired BC land

The Moha Road following the Bridge River canyon from the Terzaghi Dam to Lillooet. Courtesy of Don Swoboda

Getting to Bridge River

When mining towns opened up in the Bridge River Valley, including Bralorne, Pioneer and Minto City, the best way to get to the valley was by boat to Squamish on the Union Steamship Line, then by train to Shalalth. From Shalalth, miners and others would take a stagecoach over Mission Mountain and into the Bridge River Valley. It took about fourteen hours if there weren't any obstacles, such as rockslides.

The Pacific Great Eastern Railway line from Squamish to Lillooet was completed in 1915. The First World War got in the way of further expansion — no steel or manpower was available for those years. When the PGE resumed in 1923, it was extended northward to Quesnel. North Vancouver wasn't connected until 1956 and diesel Budd Cars were introduced to the line. The amount of time it took to get to Shalalth was reduced by half.

In order to bring a car into the Bridge River Valley, it would have to be loaded onto a scow (a flat-bottomed boat) at Craig Lodge, at the Lillooet end of Seton Lake, where it would be towed up the lake to Seton Portage. The scow service was run by a man named Frank Durban. At Seton Portage the car drove off the scow and over the mountain. Winters with temperatures below freezing would make the journey much longer, especially when Seton Lake froze over and had to be broken up with sledgehammers.

Durban's scow was replaced by a ferry service for a handful of years, but that was discontinued by 1935, when the PGE introduced a flatcar service between Shalalth and Lillooet. Cars were driven onto the flat car, which was pulled by a gasoline-powered engine — the "gas car" — along the shores of Seton Lake, to Lillooet, about 18 miles (30 km). The gas car made two runs a day, and then only one run each direction in the later years. Drivers had to make a reservation or risk being stranded for the night in Shalalth or Lillooet. The gas car also served to transport passengers and grocery orders from everybody's favourite general store, Yada's, to Shalalth for pickup.

The mining towns were only accessible by long and difficult roads. After a plane crash in 1953, in which an injured miner, a nurse and two other passengers crashed into the side of Cheakamus Mountain, the government finally decided to build a proper road to connect the isolated communities with Lillooet. With the help of Minister of Highways Phil Gaglardi, managers of the Bralorne and Pioneer mines, and other committee members, the 15-mile (24-km) road was built through the narrow canyon, connecting the Mission Dam (now Terzaghi Dam) with the old Moha Trail, which was established by the St'át'imc over generations and had been used back in the day for mining operations.

Staff located in Vancouver whose expertise was critical to the project flew into Bridge River in the company's Grumman Goose aircraft. The aircraft could make the trip in a matter of hours, which was preferable to the day-long trip by land.

surveyor Barry Cotton. "Let's not forget, there were no modern conveniences such as mucking machines, just a lot of men with shovels filling up the handcars to push back out to the portal."[4]

Early on, the miners used only candles to light their way. By the 1930s, to illuminate the work underground, the men used open-flame carbide lamps that were also used in nearby mines — a temperamental device that often went out at crucial moments. The lamps had water and carbide chambers and burned on acetylene gas that was created when the water dripped into the carbide. The men carried little cans of carbide on their work belts. When their lights burned out, they'd ask another worker to shine a light their way while they reloaded the carbide into their lamp, which was worn on a bracket around a hardhat or cap. They'd unscrew the base of the lamp, dump out the white residue, and reload with carbide, then top up the water chamber and light the lamp with a cigarette lighter–style flint and wheel. Sometimes, everybody's lamp would be out and they'd have to reload their lamps in total darkness. It wasn't until 1936 that carbide lamps were replaced with battery-powered lamps that could last twelve hours.[5]

ABOVE The Budd Car provided daily service between North Vancouver and Lillooet in the 1960s. Budd Car service ended in 2002. Courtesy of the Royal BC Museum

BCER employee John Purchas recalled going to visit the Seton Lake site to play against the Bridge River basketball team, around 1930. The tunnelling was still underway, and he remembered walking into the middle of the mountain: "We went in both sides, they took us around. It was snowing on one side, and bright sunshine on the other. But they took us in, and it was scary."

Meanwhile, in more genteel surroundings, the plush eastern offices of enterprising men, the BCER's great schemes had attracted attention. In the spring of 1928, a new Montreal-based syndicate successfully mounted a hostile takeover of the BCER (there had been several attempts). Many of the men in the syndicate had been involved in the 1920 purchase of Bridge River Power, before Horne-Payne and Barnard intervened. But apparently their interest had not waned. One of them, Arthur Nesbitt, was co-founder of Nesbitt, Thomson & Company. He had formed the Power Corporation of Canada in 1925, a holding company he co-owned with his business partners Peter Thompson and Royal Bank of Canada president Sir Herbert S. Holt, among others. They were especially focused on the acquisition of utilities. They would turn BCER into the fifth-largest corporation in Canada, with total assets of nearly $700 million.

On May 19, 1928, they incorporated a new company as the BC Power Corporation Limited (the Power Corporation), which it would remain for its existence. The Power Corporation became holder of all common shares of the subsidiary BCER. Holt—one of Canada's richest men at the time, if not the richest—purchased 85 percent of the BCER stocks. A civil engineer who had been knighted in 1915 for his part in designing the rail network that supplied ammunition to the front lines during the First World War, and who gave Britain a full squadron of Spitfires early in the Second World War, Holt was not only the Royal Bank of Canada president but also the co-founder and president of Montreal Light, Heat & Power. He sat on the boards of more than 200 companies, including Shawinigan Water & Power, the largest electricity supplier in Canada. Because of his ruthlessness, the Irish businessman was despised in Montreal, where he lived. It's not hard to understand the legendary portrayal of Holt when, nearing the end of the Depression, he was famously quoted as saying: "If I am rich and powerful, while you are suffering the stranglehold of poverty and the humiliation of social assistance; if I was able, at the peak of the Depression, to make 150% profits each year, it is foolishness on your part, and as for me, it is the fruit of a wise administration."[6]

Horne-Payne was quite ill at this point, and hadn't long to live. He reluctantly resigned from BCER after thirty-one years, and wrote a letter of farewell to president Kidd. He and his long-time business colleague Barnard, with whom he'd founded the company, couldn't complain. They were exceedingly wealthy and would become even wealthier after the purchase. Barnard was also nearing the end of his life, and would die a few years later. But their belief in Bridge River had paid off: the eastern syndicate paid $60 million to the shareholders for BCER.

By the end of 1928, Kidd would also step down as president, accepting chairmanship of the BC Power Corporation's board and turning over the helm to W.G. Murrin. Kidd was not in alignment with the new board's decision to shelve the Bridge River project, however. There had long been reluctance to take on such a major project so far from the growing urban centre of Vancouver. In a February 1925 memo to Kidd from company electrical superintendent J.I. Newell, the engineer wrote: "The magnitude of the work ahead naturally demands caution and the most thorough investigation . . . I feel strongly that the company would be in a much more favorable position to deal with the Bridge River development if the Ruskin power plant were built first, and a certain amount of additional steam plant capacity installed in Vancouver."

FACING A Grumman Goose aircraft used to bring staff to projects floats on the water in front of the Bridge 1 powerhouse. Courtesy of BC Hydro Library and Archives, Jack Lindsay Photographers Limited

had a fifteen-year inventory of inflows, with monthly and yearly flows of Bridge River and its tributaries. The data showed him that the flow was subject to the seasons, with a low water flow occurring in the winter months of January, February and March, when temperatures dropped below zero. By April, the waters gradually rose and increased through to early July, at their maximum. They then slowly dropped in August and September and held until the cold set in by late December. The flow was different from the coastal systems reliant on rain. Bridge River flows stayed strong, which meant they would complement the existing Buntzen system. Between them, the Lower Mainland would be provided with consistent, reliable power.

Carpenter identified one of the biggest challenges to the project, which was the site for a lower storage dam. BCER had spent the years from 1922 to 1926 — prior to the takeover of Bridge River Power — searching for a section of riverbed with a suitably stable foundation, spending thousands of dollars conducting drilling tests in the canyon below the basin. And although the mountains that towered over the channel were made of solid granite, the riverbed held so many loose layers of gravel and sand as to make damming difficult. (This would become a problem that could only be solved by a pre-eminent soil mechanics geologist named Dr. Karl Terzaghi. But that solution was still years away.)

Carpenter saw the development playing out over many years, depending on the economy and market demand. He had divided the project into three stages, starting with development of the diversion dam on the Bridge River, without a reservoir, and the building of the 13,200-foot (4,000-metre) tunnel with intake, surge chamber and two penstocks from the tunnel to the power station. The power station would house two 20,000-kilowatt generating units with outdoor transformers and a switchyard, a 60,000-volt transmission line running from the power station to Vancouver, and a receiving station at Vancouver. He estimated a completion date for this work by the fall of 1931. He then saw the installation of a third unit — similar to the first two — and another penstock and some additional hydraulic and electrical equipment, to be completed by 1933. He didn't see the third stage of the project — involving the building of a storage dam at or below the diversion, holding back some 750,000 acre-feet of water (an acre-foot is one acre that is one foot deep), or 925,000 cubic metres, another powerhouse, and a second tunnel west of the first one — beginning until 1938. That would bring the total capacity of the plant at that stage up to 240,000 kilowatts.

Echoing the directions of the new BCER board, he said the Ruskin Dam development on the lower Stave River took priority, estimated for completion in 1935. "This plan seems best to fit economic policies and load requirements," he wrote in his paper.

The boring of the tunnel took three years and finished on a summer evening, July 8, 1930, at precisely 8:28 p.m. Crews had worked from each end of the mountain toward the middle, and the exact moment of breakthrough was documented. It would take another year to line the tunnel with concrete. The company also had the project at the Ruskin gorge going at the same time, at a site 35 miles (55 km) east of Vancouver and two miles (3 km) upstream from the Stave River junction with the Fraser.[9] The contract for the first unit at Ruskin made headlines on February 21, 1929. It would be the third and last link of the Alouette–Stave–Ruskin group of developments, a highly ambitious and technical project. In November 1930, the Ruskin power plant opening ceremony was held on top of the hydroelectric generator, "almost the largest in the world," according to Cecil Maiden, the author of *Lighted Journey*.[10] It was attended by Premier S.F. Tolmie, Vancouver mayor William Malkin, BCER president W.G. Murrin, George Kidd and Sir Frank Barnard, the man who'd helped start it all.

By the end of 1930, the Great Depression had started to set in, although according to Maiden, the worst of it was still eighteen months away. In BC, people were still living well, and by the end of that year there were a record number of applications for motor vehicle licences, food was plentiful and reasonable, and so were clothes. The Christmas rush was a healthy one, and by January the BCER had launched its first broadcast

The Vancouver and Mainland Power Supply at a Glance

DEVELOPED	HORSEPOWER
Buntzen, Nos. 1 & 2	64,000
Stave Falls	79,000
Alouette	12,500
Steam plant	16,800
UNDER CONSTRUCTION	
Ruskin	47,000
Bridge River (one unit)	54,000
Total	**273,300**
POSSIBLE ADDITIONAL	
Ruskin	141,000
Bridge River	546,000
Grand Total	**960,300**

SOURCE: *The Bridge River Power Development*, published by the BC Electric Railway Company Limited, circa 1930.

of its *Homemakers* series on the radio, a show aimed at women that featured music and sage advice on kitchen problems.[11] By June 30, 1931, the BCER had more than 4,000 employees and many of them had purchased houses. The company had growing new demand from the consumer sector.

But by 1932, BCER had started to scale back on its streetcar service, which meant layoffs. With businesses suffering, the demand for power had diminished. The three-phase construction of the Bridge River project, as comprehensively laid out by BCER engineer Carpenter, was mothballed. About $5.4 million had been invested so far.

And then, along came a major gold rush in the Bridge River Valley. In 1933, the King vein drew hundreds of men who were desperate for work, or who were ambitious enough to mine for deposits of their own, to the mines at Bralorne and Pioneer. They got there any way they could, coming from as far as Vancouver. Many of those who got to Shalalth used the BCER tunnel to walk to the valley on the other side, on their way to the mining towns. The Great Depression years of the 1930s turned out to be golden ones for BC mining — one of the few positive outcomes of the Depression was that the collapse of the world's markets had made gold, being so dependable, worth more. At the time, it was worth $40 Canadian per ounce. These were the boom years for Bralorne, which had been purchased by Austin C. Taylor and his financial backers in 1931.

(BCER's Kidd happened to be vice-president.) Bralorne was a major gold producer, and shares in the company were paying a 12 percent dividend.

The boom was on. Out of 3 million ounces of gold, an entire townsite grew, with schools, churches, bunkhouses, halls, a movie theatre, baseball teams, and powerhouses and machine shops. Seemingly overnight, the community blossomed to 1,500 people. And the economic spinoffs grew, too, including trucking, ranching and farming, and for all the shop owners and businesses in nearby Lillooet. The PGE doubled its Shalalth warehouse space by 1934, as the station there was a hub of activity. It was there that the railway's boxcars unloaded their freight, including machines and supplies. But it was also where Curly Evans loaded and unloaded his Evans Transport fleet of trucks. Evans was from the Dakotas and had arrived in the Cariboo when he was a boy, and he was a famous local, a fearless transporter who'd work through treacherous weather and mountain conditions to deliver supplies. He was also a pilot who delivered air freight, and he had an air base in Shalalth as well. Bridge River Valley gold was almost single-handedly driving the province's economy. "In many ways the thirties were the most exciting time in the community life of the Valley, as well as in the gold-mining industry," wrote Emma de Hullu, in *Bridge River Gold*.[12]

Not ones to miss an opportunity, in March 1933 the BCER board decided Bridge River was a

Evans Transport buildings in Shalalth. Evans handled virtually all of the heavy transport work including the railway siding for BC Electric during construction of Bridge 1 and 2, Mission Dam and Lajoie Dam. The company also transported materials for the mines in the upper Bridge River and hauled out their gold concentrate via the PGE Railway. Courtesy of Don Swoboda

priority, and relaunched the development there in response to the mining activity. Bralorne needed power. But the company had another motivation, too. They were on a timeline, set by the provincial government. If they wanted to preserve the water rights they held on the Lajoie Falls, on Bridge River, as well as their rights on Gun Lake, which drained into Gun Creek, a tributary of Bridge River, they'd need to begin development of the Bridge River project. As a result, the defunct Bridge River townsite became active again, and the Shalalth stop became the PGE Railway's busiest.

BCER assigned Vancouver builder E. Thomas a contract for clearing the transmission line right-of-way. By 1934, plans and preliminary fieldwork were underway for a 4,600-horsepower generation plant on Seton Lake, as well as a 53-mile (85-km) 60,000-volt transmission line through the Bridge River Valley, to serve several mines in the area.

The decommissioned Jordan River Unit No. 1 on Vancouver Island was dismantled and brought in and reassembled at the Bridge River site. It was installed inside a modest, temporary powerhouse dating back to 1927 that had housed the diesel generator supplying the mines at Bralorne. Instead of building a diversion dam for the temporary unit, a small crib structure was built on the Bridge River and water was pumped from a canal through the tunnel intake. Water was then drawn through a temporary 24-inch (60-cm) pipe inside the tunnel that connected to a 24-inch (60-cm) penstock that dropped steeply down to a turbine on the shore of Seton Lake (the old penstock is still there today). In order to get a transmission line across the Bridge River, one of the engineers working on the line had a novel suggestion: fly it across using a kite. The engineer was an experienced kite flyer, so he oversaw the creation of a six-foot (1.8-metre) kite that was rigged to carry a light line. With the help of a prevailing wind, he flew the kite to the opposite shore and within a mere 30 feet (9 metres) of where they needed it to land. Once secured, the light line was used to carry a heavier line that could be used to pull transmission line cables over the river.[13]

The temporary power plant—which wouldn't interfere with future plans to install permanent units at Bridge River that would power the Lower Mainland—would be completed by the end of July 1934.[14]

By September of 1933, the Depression was at its worst, although eastern Canada was showing some economic vitality. BCER president Murrin stated

Dal Grauer Represents the Next Generation

Dr. Albert Edward "Dal" Grauer was a Rhodes scholar and celebrated economist. He was born on Sea Island on January 21, 1906, where his parents Jacob and Marie had been pioneer settlers. He went on to earn a first class honours degree in economics and history when he graduated from UBC, at age nineteen. He then earned a bachelor of arts in jurisprudence from University College, Oxford, which he attended as a Rhodes scholar, before earning his PhD in economics and political science from the University of California, Berkeley. It was at Oxford that he became captain of Canada's lacrosse team and competed in the 1928 Olympics in Amsterdam, alongside his brother Carl. He also obtained an honorary law degree from UBC. He returned to Canada in 1931 and worked as a lecturer at the University of Toronto, then became the youngest full professor in Canada in 1937 when the university eagerly offered him the position of associate professor of its social science department, and then the position of department director.

Dr. Grauer was soon hired away from his career in academia. In 1939, at age thirty-three, Grauer joined the BC Electric Railway Company as general secretary, but within seven years he would become president and chairman of the company. With a renewed labour force that had just returned from war, one of Grauer's first goals as president of BC Electric was to finally complete the Bridge River generating station — the biggest hydroelectric power development at the time in the province. It was also the most ambitious, because of the incredibly rugged terrain, brutal winters and the challenge of trucking materials over the 4,000-foot (1,200-metre) Mission Mountain, with the road's numerous switchbacks.

Under his guidance, the company also embarked on an era of major expansion of hydro-electric and natural gas development, propelled by a growing population that needed power. Under Grauer, BC's hydroelectric generation capacity more than tripled. He also pioneered a 138,000-volt underwater transmission cable electrical connection to Vancouver Island.

Grauer sat on the board of major businesses, such as the Royal Bank of Canada, the Ford Motor Company of Canada and California's Pacific Gas & Electric. He sat on the boards of the Vancouver General Hospital and the Vancouver Symphony Society, and had a deep appreciation of UBC, architecture and the arts. He joined the Royal Commission on Canada's Economic Prospects, which had come out of a 1955 draft article by Walter Gordon that questioned government policy, such as selling off Canada's natural resources and businesses to foreigners, particularly Americans. The study was a massive undertaking that was completed in eighteen months and forecast population growth, labour force size and sectors of the economy. The commission also made over fifty proposals, almost all of which were incorporated into legislation.

in a speech that he expected the same improvement to make its way to BC. In the spring of 1936, Barnard, co-founder of the company, died in Victoria. He had become Lieutenant-Governor of the province in 1914 and was knighted because of his service through the war years. The company was moving into an era with a younger group of executives at the helm. In August 1939, Albert Edward "Dal" Grauer joined the company at age thirty-three, and he was considered a catch because of his already impressive credentials. On top of a remarkable academic career, which included running the social science department at the University of Toronto, he had served as an expert for the landmark Royal Commission on Dominion–Provincial Relations, among other achievements. He was also a local, having grown up in the Vancouver area and attended UBC, and he returned to BC when offered the general secretary position at BCER, overseeing the Public Utilities Commission data.

Aspirations were high, but when Grauer joined the BCER the country was already deep into the Second World War. The company was heavily involved in the war effort, with some employees sent off to battle, and those at home

ABOVE Bridge River's first hydroelectric powerhouse. In 1932, a Jordan River hydro generating unit was brought in from Vancouver Island to serve as the temporary supply for the mines at Bralorne. Bridge 1 had not been built yet, and power was carried over the mountain on a 60-kilovolt power line to the Bralorne, Pioneer and Minto mines. Courtesy of BC Hydro Library and Archives

Turbine Technology

The use of water to generate power is nothing new, and started with the wooden water wheel, most often used to mill grain. Like the modern hydroelectric turbine, the ancient water wheel depended on the movement of water. The water wheel was invented about 4,000 years ago in Greece, and involved blades or buckets that would turn from the weight of flowing water.

Sometimes, the stream would be dammed and a millpond would form a reservoir, which would be used as needed. The channel water that feeds the mill is called a headrace; water that leaves the wheel is called a tailrace. Credit for widespread use of the industrial water wheel in the mid-eighteenth century goes to the British father of civil engineering, John Smeaton, whose breastshot water wheel design played a huge role in driving the Industrial Revolution. Smeaton had discovered that water wheels were most efficient when the water entered high on the wheel, as opposed to the undershot type, which is powered by natural water flow.

Technology is always morphing into something more efficient, and in 1827 French engineer Benoît Fourneyron had discovered that smaller horizontal wheels, or turbines, were more efficient than the water wheel. Unlike a water wheel, a turbine could handle water falling under pressure from a great height, or head.

In order to generate electricity, the rotation of magnets is required. The rotation produces alternating current (AC) in the generator coils. It is in the generator that electricity is produced, where the kinetic energy of the dropping water is converted to electrical energy. The drop of the water, or the head, combined with the volume or flow, determines the amount of electricity generated.

British engineer James Francis, who'd immigrated to Lowell, Massachusetts, drastically improved upon the turbine and published his

Jim Gemmill with writer Kerry Gold (*right*) and Bryan Bodell (*left*) examining the display of a Pelton turbine in the proximity of Seton powerhouse. Courtesy of Don Swoboda

findings in 1855. His Francis turbine is still widely used today. Francis turbines, generally referred to as "reaction turbines," are in service at the Seton and Lajoie generating stations.

In the 1870s, Lester Pelton of Ohio developed the Pelton wheel, an impulse water turbine that has nozzles directing high-pressure water onto "buckets" mounted on a large cast wheel, angled in such a way to maximize power output. Pelton was not trained in engineering or design, but was a self-made inventor. He had participated in the California Gold Rush of the 1850s, which is where he began early explorations for his invention. Steam-powered energy had limited appeal in a mining operation since so much wood fuel was required. He figured out that a wheel that could draw from the low flow of streams could produce the most efficient energy. By the 1870s he had invented a wooden prototype, and by 1878 an iron version of his wheel was used at Mayflower mine in Nevada City. A decade later, he sold the rights to his name and patents to a company in San Francisco. The Pelton wheel became an international success story. It is most efficient when dealing with a high head and a low flow of water, which is why it's used at both Bridge River generating plants. It is generally referred to as an "impulse turbine."

working on supplying gas furnaces to the wartime shipbuilding and armament effort, and others helping to develop the War Savings Program to generate funds for the government.

Engineer Jack Steede had been with the company prior to the Montreal syndicate takeover, and he was accustomed to taking on a wide variety of assignments. Before the war there were about forty electrical, mechanical and civil engineers and twenty-five people in the electrical distribution department, with another 150 or so in the substations operations, line department and electrical shop. During the war years, staff was greatly reduced, and Steede found himself the one-man planning department, spending most of his time dealing with Ottawa on matters of materials and equipment they were allowed to purchase during a period of rationing. In 1942, Steede was made assistant to the chief engineer and helped launch the postwar planning program. The planning, he said in an interview, was "extra-curricular activity and several of us used to work at it about four nights a week."

The Bridge River townsite was once again mothballed, with only a skeleton crew left behind to maintain it. But with war, a new community would soon arrive at Bridge River, although not voluntarily.

3

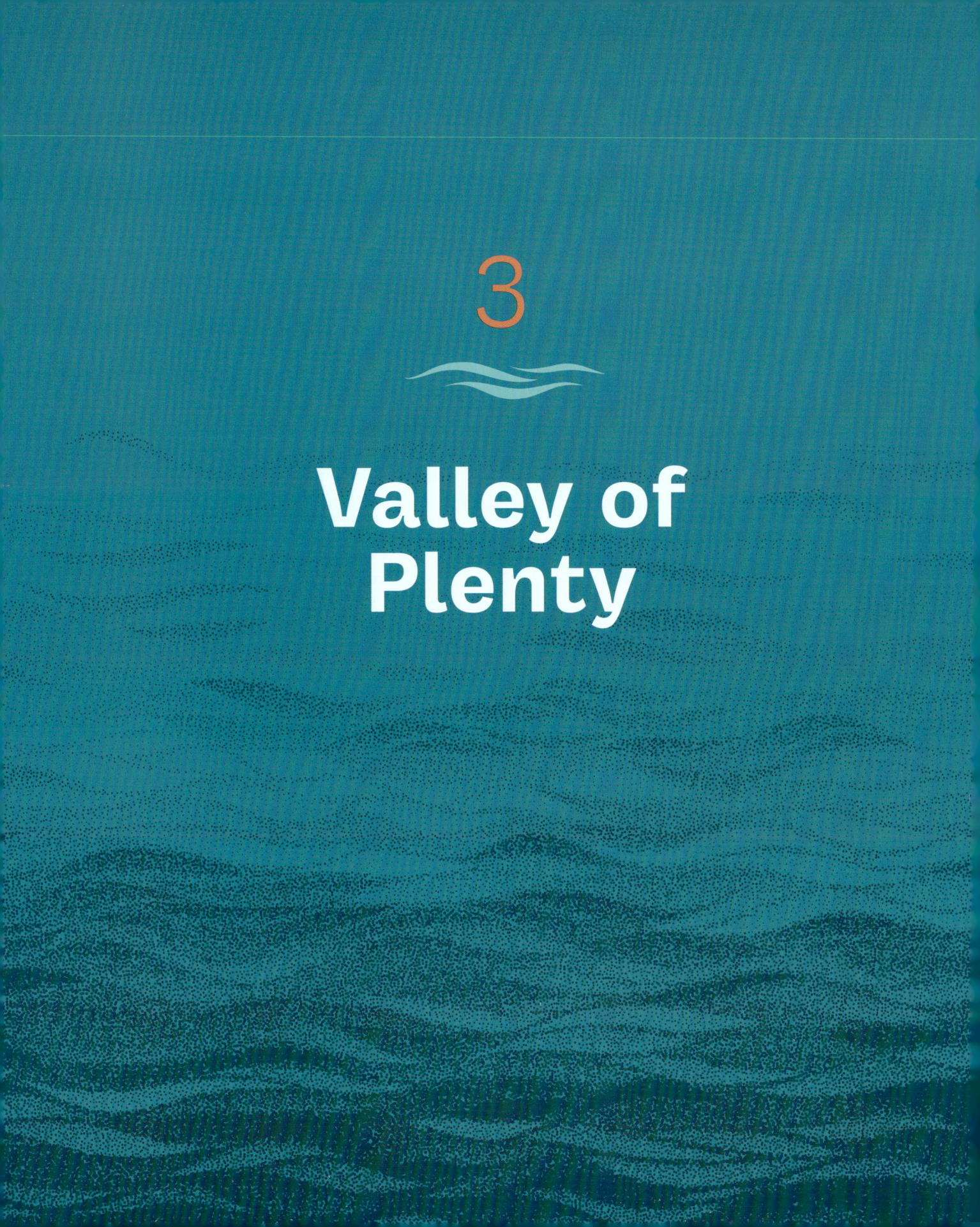

Valley of Plenty

In stark contrast to those plush offices and boardrooms in big-city office buildings, where so much of BC's future was being discussed, was the day-to-day reality of the region's Indigenous communities. The St'át'imc way of life was a far different kind of prosperity, where people extracted their wealth straight from the land as opposed to paper transactions and the buying and selling of shares. Anthropologists long ago noted that prior to outside intervention, tribal cultures such as the St'át'imc were strikingly successful at meeting all their needs sustainably. Self-sufficiency had been key for thousands of years.

Within a territory they typically numbered a few thousand people, and lived in kinship-based communities of only a few hundred, according to Washington State University cultural anthropologist John Bodley. That small-scale society allowed for greater social equality and ease with which to maintain the social structure and meet their material needs. Because of their prosperous way of life, American anthropologist Marshall Sahlins, who studied Pacific cultures, once referred to tribal peoples as "the original affluent society."[1]

However, to the outsider's eye, the territory belonging to the Indigenous people may appear either unused or under-used. The outsider might also think that the tribal society has not grown its population, and therefore must be failing instead of thriving. But tribal societies that had lived within a territory for millennia understood that their population numbers were in line with what the land could offer, and that they were working in relationship to an ecosystem, not apart from it. "Their largest store of tribal wealth is in nature itself, their forests, fish, and game, and the soil and watersheds that support them," wrote Bodley in a 2005 report on the St'át'imc.[2] "This makes tribals very vulnerable to negative impacts when outsiders either extract the natural resources or reduce their access to natural resources, and most often both."

There were no conservation groups or impact studies to get in the way of major industry projects in the early days of mining, forestry and dam building. The federal government had created the Indian Act in 1876, and took control of Indigenous status, land and resources. It was therefore not too difficult for a company like the BCER to dam a river or apply to expropriate Indigenous land if it deemed it necessary.

The story of Geoffrey Downton's survey trip is well known among the Bridge River Indigenous community. His arrival is considered the turning point in their history — when white contact didn't just pass through in the chase after fur or gold, but made a claim for the watershed itself, and left its indelible mark on the valley. By the time Downton arrived, the St'át'imc were already grappling with foreigners who had been making claims to their land and resources.

The History

It was a plentiful valley, but the ancestors had their hardships, even prior to interference by white explorers and surveyors. The winters were brutal, and there were summer droughts. And neighbouring Tsilhqot'in (Chilcotin) and Sepwecemc (Shuswap) would travel over mountains and along treacherous waterways to do battle with the St'át'imc. The last battle was believed to be in about 1898. In 2003, the Tsilhqot'in and St'át'imc officially made peace and a plaque was erected at the site of the last battle, in Graveyard Valley in Big Creek Park. The two nations gathered to honour the 140 or so dead.

The St'át'imc first encountered white men when British explorers working for the Hudson's Bay Company moved their way west, looking for opportunities. In 1808, Simon Fraser made contact with the First Nations people in his search of a route to the coast, and his crew depended on members of the Dakelh (Carrier) nation to guide them through the treacherous terrain. So too did Hudson's Bay explorer Alexander Anderson in 1846, as part of the thriving fur trade that boomed from 1805 to 1855.

Although the establishment of trails and trading forts, and the mapping of the area by the British, impacted the Indigenous way of life, it wasn't until the massive Fraser Canyon Gold Rush began in 1858 that the exploits of foreigners started to truly take their toll on the Indigenous population.[3] The California Gold Rush had been going on for several years and was pretty much exhausted, so gold seekers were looking for new opportunities. When word spread about sizable gold discoveries along the Fraser River, thousands came from across Canada, the US, Europe, Britain, Australia, Mexico and China in hopes of striking it rich. By 1860, gold seekers who'd come north for the Fraser Canyon Gold Rush had discovered gold on the Horsefly River, which pushed them further north and launched the famous Cariboo Gold Rush that put Barkerville on the map. Barkerville was named after a gold prospector named Billy Barker, who'd been mining for gold in the area since 1858. He struck a gold deposit 55 feet (15 metres) deep at Williams Creek and formed the Barker Company in 1862 with a group of other Englishmen. The Cariboo Wagon Road was completed in 1865 to help pack trains get the necessary supplies to the town of Barkerville.

Suddenly, the fur-trading territories of the Tsilhqot'in and Dakelh were overrun with gold prospectors. The Indigenous people joined in the search, and in the late nineteenth century they travelled by covered wagon to work in established mines and worked their own placer mines along the rivers. Many of them became highly skilled gold miners.

Stories of men striking it rich incentivized others to follow. Towns seemed to spring up out of nothing, bringing gambling, prizefights, horse races and dance hall girls into remote regions. But towns could just as easily fade away too, which Barkerville did when the demand for gold declined.

The mode of transportation at the time was the stagecoach, a team of horses with a wagon. In the winter they'd use sleighs. In the 1860s, businessman Francis Barnard was the proprietor of an express coach service from Victoria to Barkerville, incorporated as the BC Express Company in 1871. He owned half an interest along with partners Steve Tingley and James Hamilton, who each owned a quarter. His son Frank Stillman Barnard succeeded him as president of the company. (Frank Jr. would go on to form BC Electric Railway Company with English financier Robert Montgomery Horne-Payne in 1897.)

British Columbia was truly a Wild West, with limited resources to enforce the laws. And although prospectors would come and go, the gold rushes of the nineteenth century also attracted permanent immigration and settlements. It's hard to imagine today, but the gold rush had made Lillooet the largest city west of Chicago and north of San Francisco.

The lust for gold had also turned Fort Victoria into a city, with boats arriving daily with men who had no idea how challenging the interior terrain would actually be.[4] From Victoria, it was 160 miles (250 km) to the upper Fraser, and men would get there by pack mule and anything that would float. Many never made it to the Fraser. But the ones who did worked their placer mines along Seton Lake and Bridge River, naming the gateway to the area, Shalalth, "The Mission" for the Catholic church located in the area. They climbed steep mountains and navigated rivers, enduring the sudden changes in climate, the rapids and, sometimes, starvation. It wasn't unusual for desperate men to kill their mules and horses for food.

The foreigners considered BC to be under British rule at the time, and James Douglas, who originally worked for the Hudson's Bay Company, was appointed governor of the Colony of Vancouver Island by the British government, and later the governor of British Columbia. Douglas was doing his best to exact some rules around the gold mining, but with limited success. The flood of miners had made the First Nations vulnerable to crime, starvation and disease, as the miners worked their way into their territories. The Indigenous people claimed their right to the gold and they fought back. The Haida were especially active fighting against prospectors, taking them prisoner, if need be.[5] As well, the prospecting was impacting the all-important salmon stocks, on which Indigenous people depended for survival.

Douglas wrote to the colonial secretary in London in 1857 that the nations had fought against gold prospecting on the streams that flowed into the Thompson River. He said they wanted to protect the precious gold that was part of their territory, but they also had the "well-founded impression that their shoals of salmon, which annually ascend those rivers and furnish the principal food of the inhabitants, will be driven off and prevented from making their annual migrations from the sea."[6] Governor Douglas also visited the Lillooet in 1860 and assured the communities there that the government would never take away their villages, sacred burial sites, or fishing, mining and hunting areas.

The Lillooet continued to live a nomadic life according to the seasons, as they moved between raising cows, horses and pigs; growing melons, beans, oats, hay, potatoes, barley and turnips; fishing, hunting, trapping, mining, gathering roots and berries and working for wages in their territory, to survive. To the consternation of missionaries in the region, they were highly transient people who understood the seasons and moved throughout the year. The missionaries wanted them to remain rooted on self-supporting farms, where they could integrate them with Christian customs and religion.

The Vancouver Island colony merged with the mainland of British Columbia in 1866 to form one big colony, which together became BC. Officially, the colony assumed governance over the St'át'imc territory.

Without consulting with the Indigenous people, the federal government passed the Indian Act in 1876, as the guiding document that outlined how the Dominion would interact with Indigenous groups across Canada, including the use of reserves. The aim of the act was to encourage Indigenous people to renounce their Indian status and assimilate into Canadian civilization.

Between 1881 and 1908 the Office of the Indian Commissioner and the provincial government allocated the majority of reserves throughout the province, without input from the Indigenous people. Government bureaucrats and missionaries at the time believed it was a bad idea for the Indigenous people to pursue their nomadic lifestyle.

In the late 1800s, the Lillooet people were having a particularly tough time keeping control of their territorial claims as foreign gold miners encroached. Another gold rush was underway, and foreigners were claiming stakes that included what became the highly lucrative Pioneer and Bralorne mines.

On May 10, 1911, seventeen St'át'imc chiefs came together and signed the Declaration of the Lillooet Tribe, asserting that the St'át'imc have occupied the territory since time immemorial and were the rightful owners of the land and its resources. The St'át'imc government today states:

> *The St'át'imc hold Title, rights and ownership to our territorial lands and resources. We are* ucwalmicw *(the people of the land). We are a nation, not an interest group. As proclaimed by our ancestors in the Declaration of the Lillooet Tribe, May 10, 1911: We claim that we are the rightful owners of our tribal territory and everything pertaining thereto. We have always lived in our country; at no time have we ever deserted it or left it to others. The source of these rights is St'át'imc law.*[7]

It had been a devastating few decades. The gold rush of 1858 had a disastrous impact on the First Nations, exposing them to previously unknown diseases and the threat of starvation as immigrants from around the world competed with them for food and resources. About 30,000 foreigners pushed into their lands during the gold rushes in the years following, throwing off balance their subsistence on deer, salmon and vegetation. Interior tribal populations declined by 60 percent, according to author Joanne Drake-Terry.

Many of the prospectors made land claims and set up ranches and farms of their own. Some who settled worked side by side with the Indigenous community members and established relationships. Others just saw opportunity.

In her history of the St'át'imc people, Drake-Terry noted, "Indian people were entirely self-sufficient, by fishing, hunting, and resource-gathering, farming, ranching, mining, trapping, packing, guiding, cannery work, migrant labor, logging and wood-cutting. But this balance began to change when greater numbers of new arrivals were granted tribal lands and resources by the provincial government. The Lillooet were left with their reserve allocations and little else. This meant they were very disadvantaged relative to white people in Lillooet territory."[8]

The Indigenous people of the Bridge River region did not escape the residential school system. "Most elders I know had to go through residential school and were restricted from speaking their language," says Perry Redan, former chief and Sekw'el'was (Cayoose Creek) councillor for thirty-three years. "This had a heavy impact in how they brought up their kids and the stories they didn't tell. We lost a lot of our culture because they were told to be quiet about some of our histories."

Redan was sent to residential school in Chilliwack when he was six years old. His cousins were sent to residential school in Williams Lake.

He remembers only being allowed to go home at Christmas and summer breaks. In the 1960s, the government allowed Indigenous children to attend public school. However, Redan says he went through culture shock and felt like an outsider at public school.

Throughout the years of segregation, there was an effort by Indigenous people to organize politically, but the communities were at a disadvantage. "There was a political organization out there working on these issues, but not many, because populations were down," says Redan. "We went through all manner of struggle at the time."

The Salmon

Bridge River joins the Fraser River near Lillooet, a hugely important salmon fishing site for the First Nations. Salmon were plentiful in the lakes, rivers and streams of the area, and the St'át'imc relied heavily on the supply.

In the summer, the St'át'imc would go into the hills to gather wild carrots and onions, flowers like balsamroot and glacier and chocolate lilies, and serviceberries, salal berries and huckleberries. In winter they would trap beaver and martin and hunt for mountain goats and mule deer.

But because they could fish throughout the year, salmon and trout were the main food source for the St'át'imc. The Tsal'alh fished on Seton Lake and on Portage Creek between Seton and Anderson Lakes, and the Xwisten fished on the upper part of Bridge River, while the Sekw'el'was fished for trout on Cayoosh Creek. In the early nineteenth century, they'd use bag nets or dip nets to catch fish on the Fraser River between Lillooet and Fountain, dipping them into the dark eddies where the fish would take a break on their journey through the rapids. They'd catch small sockeye fry and trout near lake outlets using basket traps. Springtime salmon fishing was done from a fishing platform built out over the water and staked out by an individual or family, who would often share the perch with others. There were also sites along the sides of the Fraser River and Bridge River Rapids that were for public access, for neighbouring communities.

The St'át'imc would fish the lakes and rivers year-round, but the biggest run was in the late summer, when the adult Pacific salmon were at their peak on their return from the ocean. Once they returned to the river from their sea journey as adults by summer's end, fishers were waiting for them. Each family had claim to their own campsite, with fish drying racks on the riverbanks, where they'd be set up for the season. The racks would soon fill with rows of drying fillets hanging in the sun, to serve as a rich source of protein and omega-3 fatty acids for the harsh winter months ahead.

St'át'imc First Nation member John Bull with two large chinook salmon, circa 1902. Courtesy of the Royal BC Museum

It was a tradition for families to spend several weeks camped out by the river to catch fish and dry them on the racks. The weeks spent by the river allowed for stories to be told by the elders and for community members to share information and to bond.

In the fall, the salmon would return, tired and bloated on their exhausting journey upstream to the riverbed where they had begun life, and turn a bright red, a signal that they were ready to spawn — the final stage in their life cycle. Thousands gathered against each other in the riverbeds, turning the waters a roiling, shocking crimson colour, as the females wriggled and released their eggs into the gravel to be fertilized. By spring, the eggs would hatch and begin the life cycle over again.

Lajoie Dam upstream held back the water to form Downton Lake Reservoir, which covers 5,600 acres (2,200 hectares) of former valley. A few miles downstream, the Mission/Terzaghi Dam held back the water to form Carpenter Lake Reservoir, another 11,000 acres (4,600 hectares). To put the size in perspective, consider that Vancouver's Stanley Park is approximately 980 acres (400 hectares) and New York's Central Park is 840 acres (340 hectares). The river water was diverted through Mission Mountain, which some say was named after Tsal'alh chief Mission Peter, who was one of the signatories of the Lillooet Declaration of 1911, according to former Tsal'alh chief Ida Mary Peter. It's believed that Mission Peter, a Bridge River supplies packer, lived to 117 years.[9]

Gerald Michel, a soft-spoken man nicknamed BoBo, is the lands and resources coordinator for the Xwisten (Bridge River) Band, and he says he feels a particular love for the river that other fishery workers don't often share. For the last twenty years, he's worked as a field technician taking stock assessments of the fish.

VOICES FROM BRIDGE RIVER

In the old days, he says, the community used to pull 70- or 80-pound (30- to 35-kilogram) white-fleshed chinook from Bridge River prior to the Lajoie and Terzaghi Dams. There was never any need to fish on the Fraser. In the old days, the St'át'imc estimate that at least 20,000 salmon spawned in the Bridge River. Today, it's estimated that fewer than 1,000 return to spawn. Michel can give you the numbers of chinook, coho and steelhead trout smolt stocks per year off the top of his head.

Standing at the side of the Fraser River on a chilly October day, the campsites are empty at the end of the fishing season. He says there are sixty camps on the west side of the river and another forty-five on the east side. "Most of the camps down there belong to Mount Currie people," he says, pointing. "There are Pavilion, Fountain and Seton people there too, they're all mixed in."

Today, families continue to gather to fish and hang the salmon to dry on racks in their campsites, along the banks of the Fraser River, close to a junction with the Bridge River. The younger generation continues to learn fishing skills, using gill nets at the water's edge.

"It big-time changed," says Darwyn John, who was raised on the Shalalth Reserve in the 1950s and 1960s. "There were so many fish you felt like you could walk across the lake," he says. "From my recollection, we lost many species of fish from Seton Lake in that time. You could start fishing in May and there was no break in

46

FACING Today, St'át'imc communities continue to fish their traditional territories. Pictured is Marcel Adrian, with a sockeye salmon caught in the Fraser River, on the Xwisten fishing grounds. Courtesy of Jack Edwards BELOW A drying rack for air drying salmon located at T'it'q'et, on the bank of the Fraser River near the confluence with the Bridge River. Courtesy of Sid Scotchman

fish runs. Now, you fish for a while, then no fish, then another run." When he was small, his family travelled everywhere by boat because they didn't own a car. The water of Seton Lake was so clear you could drop a tin can down into it and watch it sink all the way to the bottom. He remembers when the dam opened, standing on the Seton lakeshore with his mother and father. The kids hadn't been allowed near the construction site because of all the trucks and machinery. He would have been about five years old, and he didn't understand what all the excitement was about that day. He heard the blast of a horn, and he saw "a great big brown snake of mud that went across the lake from the powerhouse. It followed the channel all the way to Lillooet. It changed the lake entirely for about a year, and then we started getting that present glacial colour."

He was also about five years old when they got electricity at their house. It materialized as a single light bulb that hung from the ceiling of each room. He didn't see television until age ten. The walls of his house in Shalalth were filled with sawdust, and the attic was insulated with piles of Eaton's catalogues.

The reconstruction of traditional pit houses at Keatley Creek. Gerald Mitchell is explaining the site to the Power Pioneers book team, joined by Elder Carl Alexander (Xwisten) on the right (in the safety jacket) and St'át'imc spokesman Rod Louie at the back of the group. Courtesy of Jim Gemmill

(keek-willy) holes, with many ranging 30 to 65 feet (9 to 20 metres) in diameter. The pit houses were lined with cedar bark and had roofs built out of radial poles of wood, covered with grass sod or hides for insulation. A hole in the middle offered ventilation for a central cooking fire. Several families lived in each of these winter structures, which dotted the entire area at one time. The Xwisten (Bridge River) community plans to rebuild several of the pit houses, or kekuli holes, to educate their children, as well as visitors from afar, about the lives of their ancestors. One of them is currently being reconstructed, and has its timber roof already in place.

An elder named Carl Alexander lives near the site, so he's a frequent visitor. Alexander was born in 1941 and grew up in a log house on 125 acres (50 hectares) of land, about 20 miles (30 km) outside of Shalalth. As soon as the ground thawed out, his family would plant carrots, potatoes and corn, he says. They stored potatoes in the cellar under the house and in cellars out in the gardens, burying them deep enough that they wouldn't freeze. They'd trade their bounty for a sack of rice or flour. His mother would wash their clothes by hand, because they didn't have electricity. In winters, they had fires going all night long, and he started packing wood as a toddler. At six he trapped squirrels, and when he was older he trapped martin, mink and beaver, later pulling in a decent living of around $500 a month during trapping season with his own trapline.

"Our house was always full of people," Alexander says. "All the relatives and the people from the communities of Seton Portage and Shalalth would come up to visit and hunt. It was a good life. I learned how to work the land." The Alexander family acreage was one of many properties expropriated for the Bridge River project, and was flooded when the dam was built.

The St'át'imc often went to work for the new industries that moved into the territory. The teenage Alexander went to work for BCER, using machetes and axes to slash the route for the power line from Darcy to Birken. He went on to do contract work for logging companies, making $600 a month for cutting trees to length. He worked on the PGE Railway, changing out the rail ties. But mostly, he worked as a logger until 1980, and then he got his industrial first aid certificate and worked at the sawmill in Lillooet for seventeen years.

He'd like to go back to live around Jones Creek, not far from the family farm, but says, "I'm getting up in age, and I can't do very much anymore. I only go home when I have to, and this is my home now."

He talks about relatives who also had to move from their homes for various reasons: "My cousin Francis Paul, he had to move out of the area where the penstock goes. Tommy Bull, he completely lost his place. He had a place next to Francis and Emily Paul. They moved Emily from their orchard further up the mountain there, where they have the school now in Shalalth. On the east side of the pipes that cross the road, you can still see the apple trees she had up there."

4

Bridge River Internment Camp

On December 7, 1941, Japan bombed Pearl Harbor, followed by an attack on a base in Hong Kong. Canada and other nations declared war on Japan. In North America, people of Japanese ancestry were suddenly the enemy, and the government took swift action on moving them to internment camps. Prior to their removal, they'd heard rumours of the government seeking their evacuation, but the Japanese community didn't think it was possible. The community had even done its best to assuage the fears of non-Asians by buying $300,000 in victory bonds. But with war officially declared, the government created a 100-mile (160-km) security zone along the west coast, from which all ethnic Japanese people were forcibly evacuated.

Prior to the Second World War, BC was home to about 22,000 Japanese Canadians, who were mostly new arrivals or first generation. (First generation Japanese are called Issei and second generation are Nisei.) Thousands of Japanese people, whether Issei or Nisei, were removed from their homes and interned in camps and on farms, mostly in BC's interior and Alberta. The government funded the internment program by selling off the homes, cars, fishing boats and other assets that belonged to the Japanese Canadian community. In her book on the internment, historian Ann Gomer Sunahara writes: "Not even the most pessimistic had considered such an extreme measure possible."[1]

The BC Security Commission (not to be confused with the current BC Securities Commission responsible for oversight of the securities industry in BC) was created to oversee the internment program, which included a temporary processing facility at Hastings Park, in which animal barns with concrete floors were outfitted with straw mattresses and army blankets. Open troughs were to be used as toilets and showers were installed in the livestock building for women and children. The new quarters for Vancouver's Japanese community still had a lingering stench of animal urine, as well as parasites on the dirty floors, according to Gomer Sunahara. However, all levels of government were on board with the plan. The newly created BCSC advised Ottawa, and the federal government set the policy. Industrialist Austin C. Taylor was the commission's chair, and he was also the wealthy owner of Bralorne mine, located in the Bridge River Valley. Taylor would have known the Bridge River area well, which is likely how Japanese Canadians came to be interned at the nearly empty and unused Bridge River townsite, near Shalalth, as well as at Minto City, a company town near Bralorne mine where the Bridge River met with Gun Creek.

Promoter "Big Bill" Davidson, a local character who'd been working in the area since 1912, had enthusiastically planned and built the town of Minto. As the president of Minto Gold, he had big hopes for the town, and he built the streets, hotel, store and mine buildings, as well as Little Gun Lodge. He ensured the town had water and electricity from the old Bridge River hydro powerhouse by 1935. Minto never really struck gold like Pioneer and Bralorne mines, and hobbled along until 1940, eventually becoming largely vacant. Taylor, one of the wealthiest men in Vancouver, would have seen it as a perfect relocation camp for the Japanese community. In an April 1942 BC Security Commission paper, Taylor told his staff: "The Japanese are a very clean, dependable, industrious race and with kindly treatment can be guided most advantageously."[2]

The Bridge River townsite had been built in 1926 to house workers for the new power project. The 1,800-horsepower diesel plant was shut down in 1932 when the Depression hit, and the wood-frame houses, community hall, little hospital, gymnasium and tennis court remained. A skeletal operation and maintenance crew stayed on at the townsite, to run the hydro powerhouse. BCER president Murrin charged the commission $15,000 a year for the use of the townsite, and got written assurance from Taylor that the company could terminate the lease if it needed immediate use of it.

In this set of circumstances, a young Ken Yada saw his family's home and grocery store in Vancouver forcibly taken away. It was 1942, and Yada was five years old. He'd spent his childhood hanging out at the store that was attached to the family house. If a customer came in looking for Campbell's soup, he knew where to find it. His grandparents also lost the home that his grandfather had built on West Seventh Avenue, near Oak, which had a breathtaking view of the city. Today it's a designated heritage building. The Yada family was among the first Japanese Canadian families to be interned at Bridge River, and because they arrived first, they got one of the little houses. Less fortunate aunts and uncles had to live in rooms in the former hotel on the townsite. "We were lucky — we got a house," says Yada. They raised chickens in the garden and tended to a community garden where they grew watermelons and tomatoes, and as many fruits and vegetables as they could, to feed themselves. "I don't think I ate meat for a whole year," says Yada. "It was tough times, I know from my mom and dad. They lost everything that my dad had worked for. They worked hard."

Ritsu Saimoto arrived at the internment camp the way most everybody did, via the Union Steamship ferry at the foot of Carrall Street to Squamish, and then on to the Pacific Great Eastern passenger coach to Bridge River. Her job was to take care of her nineteen-month-old brother as she followed behind her mother, who carried their life's possessions. Her father was recovering from surgery, and was in pain. In those first few days, they slept in the hotel that had been long ago vacated by BC Electric construction workers. "We moved into two hastily partitioned rooms in the corner of the eating room," she wrote of that time.[3] "Rough lumber was used and I remember peeping through the knotholes into our neighbour's bedroom and was fascinated by the scenarios on the other side of the wall."

Everyone, she says, knew Dr. Masajiro Miyazaki, the doctor at Bridge River who treated patients far and wide, during the war and long after. Dr. Miyazaki became an icon, highly regarded by everyone because of his selfless devotion to his profession, treating patients in desperate need even if it meant he was working for free, and travelling over icy roads.

ABOVE View of west Shalalth circa 1947. Little changed during the war years when Japanese Canadians were interned there in the rows of small bunkhouses built in the late 1920s for construction workers. Courtesy of BC Hydro Library and Archives

Dr. Masajiro Miyazaki

Dr. Miyazaki was forced to give up his home at 2812 Triumph Street in Vancouver and relocate with his wife and children to the Bridge River townsite, along with the Yada family and all the other Japanese Canadian families. Dr. Miyazaki had embraced life in Canada since he'd immigrated there as a young boy. He'd joined the throng of 1,200 University of British Columbia students who'd famously participated in the Great Trek from the old Fairview campus to Point Grey, on October 22, 1922, petitioning Premier John Oliver's government to construct them a new school at the site. He was among the last class to graduate from the overcrowded Fairview building that was the early UBC. His classmates included Dal Grauer, who would become chancellor of UBC and president of BC Electric, and Walter Gage, who would become a beloved mathematics teacher at UBC and its president from 1969 to 1975. In honour of their humanitarianism, Gage would become a Companion of the Order of Canada in 1971, and Dr. Miyazaki would be appointed to the Order of Canada in 1977.

Like all people of Japanese descent in Vancouver, Dr. Miyazaki had been registered with the RCMP and issued a card number. His ID card said that he was forty-one years old, five foot six in height and 130 pounds. It stated his occupation, and showed his signature and thumbprint. The Japanese had been questioned and issued identity cards, and had also been imposed with curfews, restricting their movements at night, which meant Dr. Miyazaki's patients were vulnerable, left without twenty-four-hour care. Taylor then issued an order that made Japanese medical doctors exempt from the curfew. Dr. Miyazaki was also allowed to keep his car, unlike the Japanese who didn't practise medicine.

Near the end of July 1942, he was called into the office of the head of the BC Security Commission's medical department and told that he would be the Bridge River doctor for the Japanese internees. He was told that if he were to refuse, he'd be sent to the prisoner of war camp at Petawawa. He received assurance from a fellow Japanese internee that the community of Bridge River would look after his lodging and the cost of moving. And so, the Miyazaki family packed their car on August 5, 1942, including a cage that held a pair of bantam chickens his youngest daughter, Rumiko, couldn't leave behind.

According to a memoir by Dr. Miyazaki, 250 Japanese internees were sent to Bridge River, 300 to Minto, 300 to East Lillooet and 150 to McGillivray Falls.[4] The Bridge River internment camp was for Japanese professionals who would be self-supporting, says Dr. Miyazaki's son Ken,

Dr. Masajiro Miyazaki and his family were interned at Bridge River during the Second World War. He would later settle in Lillooet and be appointed to the Order of Canada for his service to the community. Image and consent provided by Ken Miyazaki

who was born after the war, in 1954. Ken was raised in nearby Lillooet, and eventually left for Vancouver, and would go on to work for BC Electric's successor, BC Hydro, for thirty-two years. He doesn't recall visiting the Bridge River townsite as a child. However, his much older sister Betty, now deceased, remembered growing up at Bridge River, he says. "I know it was tough living there, but at the same time, my sister had a positive attitude," Miyazaki says. "She said the funny thing is there were so many Japanese there, they outnumbered the BC Electric people. They were the majority. And I think they got along quite well.

"I remember, when we'd come to Vancouver, we would always go visit the Foxes. His name was Clifford Fox, and I forget her name. She was one of those ladies that always stood out. She had a big perm and a raspy voice like Ethel Merman. Fox was an operator in Bridge River, and they became friends with my parents and remained in contact for the rest of their lives. So even though it was an internment camp, I got the impression they mixed with the people there."

In Bridge River, Dr. Miyazaki had a three-bed hospital and handled the delivery of all the newborns. He delivered twenty-five babies at the hospital in Bridge River, two babies in Minto, nine in East Lillooet, four at a nearby reserve and three for a Caucasian family in Bridge River. He would travel on ice-slicked mountain roads in his car, or by train or even by seaplane. He would deliver a baby with only a coal oil lamp for light. On occasion, he'd treat BC Electric employees. One winter, he attended to an injured BC Electric worker at the top of Mission Mountain. It was winter, and his car got stuck, so powerhouse operator Cliff Fox drove him in his car. They spun out on the last switchback, so the two men had to climb the mountain road on foot, to the snow camp, where the snowplows were kept. Bridge River powerhouse operator Otto Hendrickson was at the top, with cracked ribs. Dr. Miyazaki taped him up and Hendrickson was well enough to help the doctor dig his car out. The two men became each other's mutual support over the episode.

The miniature castle built by Dr. Fujiwara and his son Alan near their home during their internment, which is now the site of the Bridge River Public Library. In 2011, the Bridge River townsite was completely rebuilt, and the castle was refurbished. Courtesy of Ken Yada

Hendrickson would help the doctor with his car troubles on the area's treacherous roads later, too.

The Miyazakis shared the one-level hospital building, across from the community hall where movies were shown, with dentist Dr. Asajiro Fujiwara and his family. Dr. Fujiwara had lived in Vancouver a few blocks from Dr. Miyazaki, at 3422 Eaton Street, across from Pacific Coliseum. He and his wife had a son, Alan, who was a young teen at the time.

Today, the hospital is now the Bridge River Public Library. But a white-painted miniature castle, with windows made out of the glass from antiseptic bottles, still stands in the garden, on a little hill. Dr. Fujiwara and his son Alan built the castle, which originally had water flowing around it in a moat, over a waterfall and into a pond. Flowers surrounded the castle, and it was beautiful, recalls Dave Devitt, who was born in Bridge River's House No. 8 in 1945, three houses away from the Miyazakis and Fujiwaras.

The Devitt family had arrived in Bridge River in 1934, where they settled down with seven children. Dave Devitt's father Jack had come from working at Buntzen Lake, just outside Vancouver, where he'd been an operator at the powerhouse. Dave remembers his mother consulting a big medical textbook with gory sketches when any of her children had an ailment. But like everyone in the tiny community, she relied on Dr. Miyazaki. "I was born in '45, and at that point, the Japanese were still interned there," says Devitt. "Dr. Miyazaki had become by this time a legend in Bridge River, not only for his helping the miners and helping the train workers who would get hurt, but also of course our own mechanics, and all the staff that we had. BC Electric got him all the supplies that he needed — antiseptic, bandages, aspirin, anything that was available at the time."

What Is a Snow Camp?

For many years, in the winter months, a snowplow operator would live in a house with an equipment shed at what was known as the "snow camp" at Mission summit. "During my time at Bridge, and I suspect for many years since, there was a Department of Highways camp at the peak of the road on Mission Mountain before it goes over into the Bridge River Valley or the Seton Lake Valley," explains long-time BC Hydro manager Don Swoboda, who worked at Bridge River from 1959 on and off until 1963. "It was there, I believe, to allow the snowplows to undertake their work in either direction from an 'easier' location (but still a treacherous one) that would see them starting out by plowing downhill rather than uphill, say from the Shalalth village end. The camp was critical to BC Electric in keeping the road open as far back as the 1930s, when the first, much smaller and temporary generating station was put in with a transmission line built up to Bralorne and other mines in the Bralorne area."

Keeping the road open during the construction of the modern-day facilities was also critical, as most of the supplies came in by rail to Shalalth and had to be trucked over the mountain to support construction of the Terzaghi Dam and the Lajoie Dam and generating station. The road up to the Bralorne area mines would have been a priority as well, particularly during the Second World War, when the supply of mineral products would have been essential and when there were Japanese internment camps in Shalalth and Minto City (near Bralorne). Dr. Miyazaki knew about the importance of the snow camp because he travelled the road up to Minto to service the Minto internment camp.

"Road grading would have been critical during the BC Electric construction period, from the late forties to the early sixties," Swoboda adds.

In later years, the equipment shed housed a snowcat used to service the microwave facility that provided communications between Burnaby, the Peace River and other BC Hydro facilities in the province. BC Tel and BC Hydro shared the snowcat at one point. However, the shed later burned down and the snowcat was lost in the fire.

The snow camp no longer exists because fewer people use the road than during the days when BC Hydro kept a larger crew working at Bridge River. Once the plant became automated, the numbers of residents decreased. Also, the area receives far less snow today than it did in the construction era.

The Story of Ma Murray

British Columbians of a certain age will have heard of Ma Murray, a controversial figure whose newspaper column made her famous across Canada. Margaret Murray and her husband George launched the *Bridge River–Lillooet News* in 1933, when they moved to Lillooet after George won the seat for the Liberals in that year's provincial election. He had run a newspaper in South Vancouver, and he and Margaret ran several community publications in BC.

Margaret wrote about the politics of the day in a unique, plain-talking style (she'd use made-up words like "damshur" and she didn't use punctuation), and favoured hearsay over facts. She had her share of foes as a result, but she courted the controversy. Her favourite target was the premier, W.A.C. Bennett, who she attacked relentlessly — enough so that she was taken off the guest list for a 1965 dinner to be held in Vancouver for Bennett, to which she was accidentally invited. "They're chicken!" she wrote.

Margaret Theresa Lally had come to Canada from Kansas, where she'd worked as a young bookkeeper in a saddle-making factory. She'd slip notes inside the saddles they shipped to Alberta, trying to strike up correspondence with a cowboy. She got several letters in return, so she and her sister headed to Canada in 1912 to land cowboy husbands. But they needed money, so they stayed in Vancouver. Instead, she met George Murray when she got a job at his little newspaper, the *Chinook,* and soon after they were married.

In 1933, George was offered the Liberal nomination in Lillooet, a mining and logging town 250 miles (400 km) north of Vancouver. They found a place over one of the taverns, and began campaigning on promises of a highway to Alaska.

They won the election and launched the *Bridge River–Lillooet News*. They bought a building on Main Street and brought in a press from Vancouver. The paper soon sold almost 2,000 copies a week, and their two children worked as reporters. When times were tough, they'd let their advertisers in town pay with pies and chickens.

After war broke out, more than 1,000 Japanese internees were relocated to the Lillooet area. Ma Murray became an outspoken opponent of having them in the town, and published articles with headlines such as "Japanese Forced on Lillooet Area — Citizens Bow in Disgrace."

Looking for a new challenge, the Murrays moved to the town of Fort St. John, which was booming, and started the *Alaska Highway News*. Although the couple were diehard Liberals, Margaret inexplicably ran for the Social Credit Party, much to her family's humiliation. She lost. George won a federal seat and left for Ottawa. They sold the Lillooet paper and Margaret stayed in Fort St. John, where she was starting to gain an international reputation. But in the spring of 1959, at age seventy-one, she revived the *Bridge River–Lillooet News*. George died two years later, and Ma Murray ran the newspaper by herself, hiring her grandchildren to help. They'd write copy and she would change it all. Her contempt for Bennett and for BC Hydro became legendary. Amid reports that there was a leak in Mission Dam in May 1962, Ma Murray ventured up to the site to see the dam and the lake level for herself. In her inimitable style she reported on the lake level to the *Province* newspaper: "It's as dry as a widow's breast."[10]

Murray received honorary degrees and became a national celebrity and a regular on TV and radio. She also was recognized as an Officer of the Order of Canada on December 18, 1970. She eventually sold the paper but continued as a weekly columnist until age eighty-five. She died in 1982 at ninety-four and was buried in Fort St. John next to her husband.

Ma Murray in her office at the *Bridge River–Lillooet News*. Courtesy of the Royal BC Museum

5

The Construction Era

"For the past three years, a tremendous new surge of activity to produce wealth from these wild and majestic mountains has been underway; not wealth from their ores this time, but wealth from the snow fields on their lofty crests that melt to form the Bridge River. For the waters of Bridge River — harnessed and tamed by man — are to produce electricity, the cheap and forceful servant of man, that will insure the industrial area of the Lower Mainland an ample supply of electricity for the factories moving to, and being built in, B.C."

— BCE NEWS —

The Bridge River project had supplied crucial power to the mining industry, as well as jobs, in the war years. The tunnel that connected Bridge River with Seton Lake was supplying water to a small generating unit. The unit powered the Bralorne and Pioneer mines about 40 miles (65 km) up the Bridge River Valley. The BCER had secured the right-of-way for a future transmission line to Vancouver in the mid-1920s. Once completed, the Bridge River project would tie in with the Stave–Ruskin and Buntzen facilities, supplying the growing Vancouver region with its domestic and industrial electrical needs for the next two decades, into the late 1960s.

By April 1946, there were organizational changes and leadership shuffles at BCER. Murrin retired and Grauer became company president. In his farewell speech to shareholders, Murrin tipped his hat to his successor, assuring parent company BC Power Corporation he was confident their electrical company was in good hands as it entered the postwar years — the period when Bridge River would finally be realized as the province's largest and most complex hydroelectric project, a mammoth at 600,000 horsepower, once fully built out. The project would generate more power for BC than Niagara Falls would for Ontario.[1] The company was hopeful at war's end, and ready to get back to work.

Also at this time, the BC Power Corporation split the BCER into three separate, wholly owned companies. The BC Electric Company Limited (BCE) oversaw the generation and transmission of electricity, as well as the manufacture and distribution of coal gas in Greater Vancouver and Greater Victoria. The BC Electric Railway Company (BCER) took over all distribution of electrical energy on the mainland and southern Vancouver Island, as well as transit operations in those regions, and interurban rail on the mainland, for freight and passengers. And BC Motor Transportation Limited was responsible for the interurban bus operation in the Lower Mainland. From here on, the BCE would be responsible for Bridge River and all other hydroelectric projects in the company's growing network.

But it would be a period with growing pains, too, because along with the substantial postwar growth came a new political mood in the province. The Second World War had changed the dynamic: demand for electricity skyrocketed. And the company wasn't at the ready to answer it.[2] People had new expectations. And the new guard of politicians wasn't as easily going to abide by the reign of dominance that the utility company had so far enjoyed. The period immediately after the Second World War would not be an easy one for BCE. In 1946, there was a major movement underway to bring more power to the southern region of the province. The war was over, the economy was strong and citizens were getting more than a little irritated that they didn't have the available power to suit their new lives. There was a general feeling that the BCE, as the chief utility provider, had played it too safe, too conservative, when it came to the electrification of the Lower Mainland. Throughout the 1930s, the utility company had added supply moderately, according to the softening demand. In 1938, only 47,000 horsepower was added to the system with the upgrade to the Ruskin Dam. And electricity rates were high. As a result, there was increasing demand by the public to expropriate the big electrical utility for the public good. The trend had already started in Quebec in 1943, when the government took over Montreal Light, Heat & Power.

A Changing Political Landscape

The connection between power and progress in BC got started prior to the end of the Second World War. The movement toward expropriation had taken hold with the provincial coalition government's creation in 1942 of the Post-War Rehabilitation Council, aimed at consulting with civic groups on the direction they felt the province should go. The electric utility was naturally a key part of the discussion. Matthew Evenden, a professor of geography at UBC, is an expert on Canadian rivers and environmental history, with a focus on the politics of hydroelectricity and the fishing industry. During the war, he says, BCE had been wary of sinking capital into hydroelectric development at a time when they feared expropriation by the provincial government. They did try to attract federal money for Bridge River during the war, using the federal interest in finding aluminum smelter sites. The majority of development back then was in Quebec, and aluminum production relied on cheap hydro. But when Alcan expanded in Quebec, the idea to bring aluminum to Bridge River fell through.

The company appealed to federal Department of Munitions and Supply minister C.D. Howe, making the case that power was a wartime necessity and they'd need funding to build the $6.5 million Bridge River project by

September 1, 1945. Howe rejected the request, deeming it unfeasible to be completed so quickly, and therefore not qualified as a "war time necessity."

The company tried again a year later, but doubling the budget. They argued for funding for massive expansion because of postwar demand. Howe once more turned the company down, only offering minor support, such as help in obtaining supplies. BCER, as it was still known, had been delivered a serious blow. By the summer of 1943 and into 1944, Vancouver was without enough power. A hot summer had left the company's reservoirs low, without the capacity to generate enough electricity. The company would have normally looked to its Vancouver steam plant at Union and Main to compensate but oil shortages made that impossible, and as a result they had to improvise by using the excess coal tar from the coal gas plant. By 1946, the company had no choice but to consider buying power from the Bonneville Power Authority in the US. The BCER also put electricity restrictions on Vancouverites.

As part of the postwar planning program, cabinet ministers and politicians travelled around the province, seeking feedback from local chambers of commerce, women's groups and a range of civic organizations. They wanted to know if they felt that BC needed a better power supply, and if so, who should supply it? The government was taking a page from Ontario's playbook on power. In that province, the Ontario Electric Power Commission had been providing power as a public service since the turn of the century. As well, all those hydro developments occurring stateside as a result of Franklin D. Roosevelt's New Deal public works programs in the 1930s, such as the Bonneville Dam, had suggested the new opportunity for provincial investment. In the US, the right wing justified state-controlled hydroelectricity as a valid means of organizing services, including road building. "For those on the left, it could be argued that it was the appropriate new way of state involvement in the economy to help organize production," says Evenden.

Another reason for producing hydropower on rivers by damming them was to reduce the risk of flooding, which was a serious threat at the time. In Oregon, the most famous example was the town of Vanport, on the Columbia River. The town had popped up during the Second World War, based on production of Boeing aircraft, and it offered the country's largest concentration of public housing for low-income workers. Almost half the population was African-American. The town was destroyed on May 30, 1948, when the Columbia River rose and broke through a railroad berm, flooding the town and wiping out thousands of homes.

The devastation led to the creation of the 1961 Columbia River Treaty, an agreement between the US and Canada to dam the upper Columbia River for flood control and shared hydroelectric power generated in the US. (The treaty led to the creation of three dam projects in Canada and one in the US.) The Bridge River was also subject to flooding, with an average rainfall of about 15 inches (40 cm) a year and an average flow of water of 3,702 cubic feet (105 cubic metres) a second, according to a company report.[3] But the river could go as high as 26,000 cubic feet (740 cubic metres) a second and as low as 164 cubic feet (4.6 cubic metres) a second, according to the company report. Flooding was, at the time, a valid fear.

One of the politicians who toured BC as part of the Post-War Rehabilitation Council was a then little-known conservative politician named W.A.C. Bennett, the future Social Credit premier who would create BC Hydro and go on to develop the Columbia and Peace Rivers. Bennett would also build highways and railways that would open up development opportunities in BC's northern Interior. Along with him was E.T. Kenney, a Liberal and the future minister of lands and forests. Kenney would help develop the controversial Nechako River Dam (later named the Kenney Dam), its associated generation plant at Kemano and an aluminum smelter project in Kitimat in the late 1940s. Harold E. Winch, head of the left-leaning Cooperative Commonwealth Federation (CCF) Party, and a booster for public power, was also in attendance.[4]

It was a travelling tour that looked a lot like an election campaign, and it proved tremendously successful in terms of public response. Using citizen feedback, the council wrote a report that reflected a desire for the state to take a postwar role in creation and distribution of hydroelectricity, which would reduce rates and service remote regions that had no power. They underscored a need to expedite the process, and to begin the work before the war had ended. They even had a budget in mind. The author of the report was a UBC professor of geology named Harry Warren, who estimated funding at about $90 million, but annual returns of $10 million on electricity sold. Warren wrote in his report that waiting until the end of the war would be too late. In terms of promoting itself to the country and the world, and realizing its full hydroelectric potential, BC was already lagging.

The push for public power had also become a rural one, and it's no wonder the majority of the outcry came from small towns and agricultural communities. The entire province paid exorbitant rates for electricity, but the rural areas were hit hardest. The government committee discovered that when compared with Ontario, British Columbians paid more than

William Andrew Cecil (W.A.C.) Bennett. Courtesy of the Royal BC Museum

twice the cost per unit of power, and used half the electricity.

With the council's report backing him, Premier John Hart issued a press release that said the province would expropriate private utilities once the war had ended, taking over power development and leaving it in the control of municipalities. Matthew Evenden says the ambiguous promise might have been a political gambit, an attempt to woo rural support in the atmosphere of an increasingly popular CCF party, which promised state ownership of power.[5]

War was a boon for the economy, with the need for armaments, ship and airplane production, as well as the workforce, which suddenly needed transit to get to and from work. In the immediate postwar climate, devastating power shortages were becoming a serious possibility, and BCER was increasingly becoming the target of public ridicule. Meanwhile, BCER directors were watching the political posturing closely.

BCER's take on the period is more optimistic, at least as written in the corporate biography, Lighted Journey. At war's end in 1945, more than 300 vets returned to their work at the company, with another 246 new hires.[6] The company had set up a new Industrial Development Department to encourage industrial growth and to convert wartime industries into everyday peacetime production facilities. Nobody wanted the economic downturn they'd experienced in the aftermath of the First World War. Howard Walters, who'd been developing War Savings for the BC government, returned to oversee the new department, which launched a now famous "Business is Moving to BC" campaign. The idea of the campaign was to stimulate development and job growth, and to advance the idea that a private utility company such as the BCER (as opposed to a publicly funded utility) was key to such growth.

Harold Merilees, who'd returned from his job as the public relations organizer for Vancouver in the National War Finance Committee, established a new Public Information department, under executive vice-president Grauer. The "Business Is Moving to BC" campaign had

Business Moves to BC

With all the current controversy, it might be difficult to believe that pipelines have been around since the 1950s. In 1951, the Parliament of Canada granted the Trans Mountain Oil Pipe Line Company a charter to construct a pipeline from Edmonton to Vancouver, with a budget of $83 million. It was part of a major industrial expansion in the province, with a host of businesses starting up within a twelve-month period.

The giant Aluminum Company of Canada (later Alcan) opened a plant in Kitimat, with the company townsite Kemano set up to build a powerhouse to power an aluminum smelter. The expenditures for the project were more than $550 million, according to a Power Corporation report from 1951.

A major pulp and paper mill opened in Prince Rupert. At that time, pulp and paper was such a big industry that pundits believed it would surpass forestry. Natural gas discoveries were well underway, with all major oil companies doing exploratory work in the north.

And shipbuilding, mining, timber, fish and, of course, hydroelectric power expansion were on the province's agenda. They were prosperous times.

ads placed in newspapers and magazines across Canada, the US and England. By the end of 1945, 594 industrial consumers had enquired about electrical service, with a projected total annual production of over $12 million.[7]

That summer, wrote *Lighted Journey* author Cecil Maiden, there were "spectacular parades and displays . . . a new friendliness and a great heartiness was flowing into the land." By the spring of 1946, Grauer was president, and his youthful informality gave the company a new image. He pressed upon his employees an open-door policy, and reminded staff that "we are living in exciting times" and "working with an exciting company."

The next year, 1947, was BCE's jubilee year, its fiftieth anniversary, so there was much to celebrate. The company spent substantial effort blowing its own horn. Past presidents Kidd and Murrin were invited to drink a toast to the occasion, and to the memory of founder Horne-Payne.[8] The BCE hired photographer Lew Parry to produce and shoot a Hollywood-quality short film called *Dinner for Miss Creeden*, complete with a script about a real-life stenographer named Flossie Creeden, who'd been one of the first female employees at the company. Grauer narrated the film, which showcased its transit, gas industry and many hydro projects, including Bridge River. Surveyor Phil Horton's mother Phyllis had a part in the film, as did many BCE employees. In 1949, the company held a screening of *Dinner for Miss Creeden* at the Stanley Theatre, followed by an Academy Awards–style ceremony. Horton remembers standing in the wings and watching his thrilled mother receive her award. In 1948, BCE released the story of its history in a book, *Lighted Journey: The Story of BC Electric*, and every employee received a copy.

The jubilee year was also when the company would begin the process of retiring the streetcar, which had been a constant presence for decades in Vancouver, New Westminster and North Vancouver. The era of the trolley bus had begun, simultaneous with the soon-to-be-realized Bridge River power project, to service this growing postwar population. Progress was very much on everybody's mind. As Maiden writes: "All the new plans of the Company would demonstrate the new concept of quicker service, faster operation and more rapid tempo."

BCE had the benefit of a wealth of experience, too. The executive was now made up of men with decades of experience under their belts, having worked on the Jordan River project, Buntzen, Ruskin–Stave Falls and Bridge River. The company supplied gas and electricity and urban trolley and motor bus systems, but also BC Motors, made up of a fleet of stage, truck and freight lines. The BCE had grown to a company of 6,000 employees with an annual payroll of $12 million.[9]

Grauer was well aware of the mood in some political quarters to nationalize the utility. Recognizing that they were now under tremendous pressure to up their game, the BCE came up with a promise to deliver $50 million in infrastructure, starting with Bridge River. While the lack of labour and supplies had sidelined the project during the war years, the company was determined to devise a major catch-up mission in the postwar years. For consumers who didn't want to take on the extra taxes that would come with public ownership, the company's ambitions to grow electrical service on its own dime would make them heroes. The company embarked on a campaign to promote domestic electricity use. A ten-year plan to finish Bridge River was compressed into a four-year crash program. With a new consumer demand for more load, the eastern owners hired the Shawinigan Engineering Company of Montreal to review and revise the original design. The Northern Construction Company and J.W. Stewart Limited would work on the construction of Mission Dam and the Bridge 1 powerhouse.

When Bridge River came out of its long hibernation in June 1946, only the concrete-lined diversion tunnel for Bridge 1 had been completed, back in 1931. The tunnel was 14 feet (4 metres) in diameter and 13,200 feet (4,000 metres) long. Survey work and acquisition of the main transmission line right-of-way via Squamish to Vancouver

They used gas-fuelled torches to burn holes into the upper parts of the sheet piles and then attached a pile extractor with jaws to pull the pilings out and to the surface. The work was so highly skilled and specialized that the divers who did it later founded a firm that built deep-sea submersibles, according to Malcolm Parry, who worked for Yves Lacroix. Lacroix, a brilliant graduate student who was writing a doctoral thesis on construction of the dam, oversaw much of the work on behalf of Terzaghi. Terzaghi only visited the dam every few weeks to inspect the progress of his revolutionary design, a design that to this day draws curious engineers from around the world.

Once the old pilings were removed, they drove new longer sheet pilings into the riverbed. Terzaghi's grout curtain went 450 feet (140 metres) down, and was 60 feet (18 metres) thick and up to 120 feet (36 metres) in length, with five rows of holes drilled into the riverbed and filled at a high pressure with the impermeable grout material, to stabilize the dam and protect against movement caused by underground water. The work was not complete until engineers were satisfied that the entire valley bottom had been sealed, recalls Parry. "That conclusion was not a ready one as such holes will always twist and divert from straight lines as the drill bits encounter harder or smaller layers of earth, boulders, and such like."

A firm called Soletanche, which had worked on grouting tests at the Aswan Dam, under Terzaghi's supervision, was contracted to do the actual sealing work. Soletanche would create "a state-of-the-art grout curtain" that would seal against any leakage all the way to the rock below the clay.[11] Parry says a sophisticated 16-mm film camera, three feet (a metre) or so long and about two inches (5 cm) in diameter, made by Longines Wittnauer was lowered into the drill holes to capture images of the instruments the holes contained, which included a compass needle with a highly sensitized pendulum. Engineers could then calculate any deviations within the drilled holes. Their aim was to create an underground pattern of holes suitable for the pressure grouting, to create a seal. They determined the nature of the seal being made within these holes by using fluorescent dye in the grout, to accurately follow its flow into the holes that had been drilled.

Construction on the dam included a spillway, which is an overflow channel that allows for the safe release of excess reservoir inflows into the river channel, to protect the structural integrity of the dam. The concrete-lined spillway carried water downstream in the channel that had been dammed. The 209,000 cubic yards (160,000 cubic metres) of rock excavated to create the spillway went into the dam itself. Any other rock required for the dam was obtained from nearby rockslides.

Sheet pilings are interlocking sheets of steel driven into the soil to prevent water leakage through the dam.
Courtesy of Mike Cleven, photographer unknown

Lajoie Storage Dam

In order to increase the output of the Bridge River plants, an additional storage reservoir for the extremely variable water runoff was built 35 miles (55 km) upstream from the Bridge 1 tunnel intake.

The site of this storage dam was at Lajoie Falls, near the mining supply town of Gold Bridge, between the upper Bridge River and what became Carpenter Lake.

Preparatory work for the dam began in June of 1947, when a camp was set up to clear the site. In 1948, the BCE had to do something about the proposed dam, which would ultimately create the Downton Reservoir, or else they would lose the water rights, which were set to expire. So that year, they began to build a rock-filled dam for storage purposes, which was finished by mid-August 1949.

But the one-unit powerhouse wouldn't get built for another seven years, until 1956. In this way, Lajoie Dam was done in two phases.

The dam was constructed out of 572,000 cubic yards (437,000 cubic metres) of rock from a nearby quarry, with a concrete intake tower built to release water from its reservoir, called Downton Lake Reservoir, into Carpenter Lake Reservoir (and later, to be used for the generating unit). The idea had been to seal the dam under a concrete coating, but engineers decided against that because they felt it could crack. Instead, the upstream side of the dam was covered in vertical timber sleepers and 4 × 12 horizontal timbers. Volcanic ash was sourced locally and spread over the timber surface to seal the dam and minimize leakage of the stored water.

In 1949, work began on increasing the height of the Lajoie Dam to a crest of 2,472 feet (753 metres) above sea level, which brought the Downton Reservoir to 2,405 feet (733 metres). The dam construction was completed by 1955, and followed by the installation of the single 22-megawatt generating unit, completed in 1956. The work coincided with installation of units at Bridge River, on the Seton Lake side of the project, to achieve maximum power production.

FACING Mel Stewart (*left*) and Doug Brunner (*right*) in front of the Lajoie Dam construction office. "Home Sweet Home" is written above the door. Courtesy of J.M. Stewart

ABOVE Raising Lajoie Dam with the low-level outlet in the foreground and the clearing of what would become the Downton Reservoir in the background. Courtesy of BC Hydro Library and Archives, Jack Lindsay Photographers Limited

VOICES FROM BRIDGE RIVER

Penstocks

Crews initially constructed two penstocks totalling about 2,100 feet (640 metres) of steel pipes dropping more than 1,000 feet (300 metres) down the mountain and crossing under the Pacific Great Eastern Railway main line, into the powerhouse. Vancouver Iron and Engineering Works manufactured the penstocks. Bridge No. 1 now has four penstocks, one for each turbine, leading from the first tunnel built in 1931. Bridge 2 has a separate water supply tunnel that splits at the tunnel portal to supply two penstocks. Each penstock splits again as it enters the powerhouse, to drive two turbines.

FACING Construction of the penstocks at Bridge 1. This specially built trolley transports each section up the mountain from Seton Lake for placement. Courtesy of BC Hydro Library and Archives

ABOVE LEFT Construction underway on a penstock at Bridge 1. The powerhouse and switchyard are visible below. Courtesy of BC Hydro Library and Archives

ABOVE RIGHT Workers bolt together a coupling on one of the penstock connections with air wrenches. The extremely steep slope they worked on would have had about a 50 percent grade. Courtesy of BC Hydro Library and Archives

ABOVE Crews work on the scroll case (which distributes water to the nozzles around the turbine) for the fourth generating unit at Bridge 1. Courtesy of BC Hydro Library and Archives, Jack Lindsay Photographers Limited

FACING Transmission survey crew on the initial 230-kilovolt line from Bridge River to Burnaby. Courtesy of BC Hydro Library and Archives

For engineers, it's all about efficiency and maximizing the output. You want to save the precious water stored in a reservoir, because in the dry season the inflow will be much less. In the Bridge River Valley, the glacier runoff that melted in the spring had to be carefully managed ahead of the dry winter months, when most everything froze and river flows dropped.

Map of the Seton River and the Seton power canal between Seton Lake and the Fraser River. The Seton Dam is equipped with a fish ladder. The upper and lower spawning channels are on the river with the power canal in the foreground and the Seton powerhouse on the shore of the Fraser River. Courtesy of the Adult Fish Passage Monitoring Program 2015, University of British Columbia

VOICES FROM BRIDGE RIVER

OVERVIEW OF SETON POWER PROJECT

- Upper Spawning Channel
- Lower Spawning Channel
- Power Canal
- Fraser River
- Seton Powerhouse

The next phase of construction involved more power lines to service the Lower Mainland, as well as substations to step down the voltage of power travelling down those lines to service homes, businesses and industries. In 1960, about 300 miles (480 km) of transmission lines were constructed in BCE's service area and eleven new substations were added to the network.

BCE was also busy that year extending the gas system as demands for natural gas grew. Crews were busy installing 200 miles (320 km) of gas pipeline to new home connections. The company was also busy expanding urban transit and inter-urban transit networks. It spent millions of dollars in capital costs, developing urban infrastructure.

ABOVE Aerial shot of Seton headworks looking west toward Seton Lake with the canal on the left, the dam in the middle and the Seton River on the right. The area between the canal and the river is where the first spawning channel was built in 1969. Courtesy of BC Hydro Library and Archives, photo (detail) by Parry Films

FACING TOP The Seton Canal headworks looking downstream with the canal on the right, the (funnel-like) fish ladder next to the syphon white water spill and the Seton Creek channel on the left, 1981. Courtesy of BC Hydro, photo by Glynn Morris

FACING BOTTOM Two penstocks supply water to the four turbines in the Bridge 2 powerhouse (*upper left*). The Bridge River Terminal substation is to the upper right. Picture taken from the second tunnel portal. Courtesy of Don Swoboda

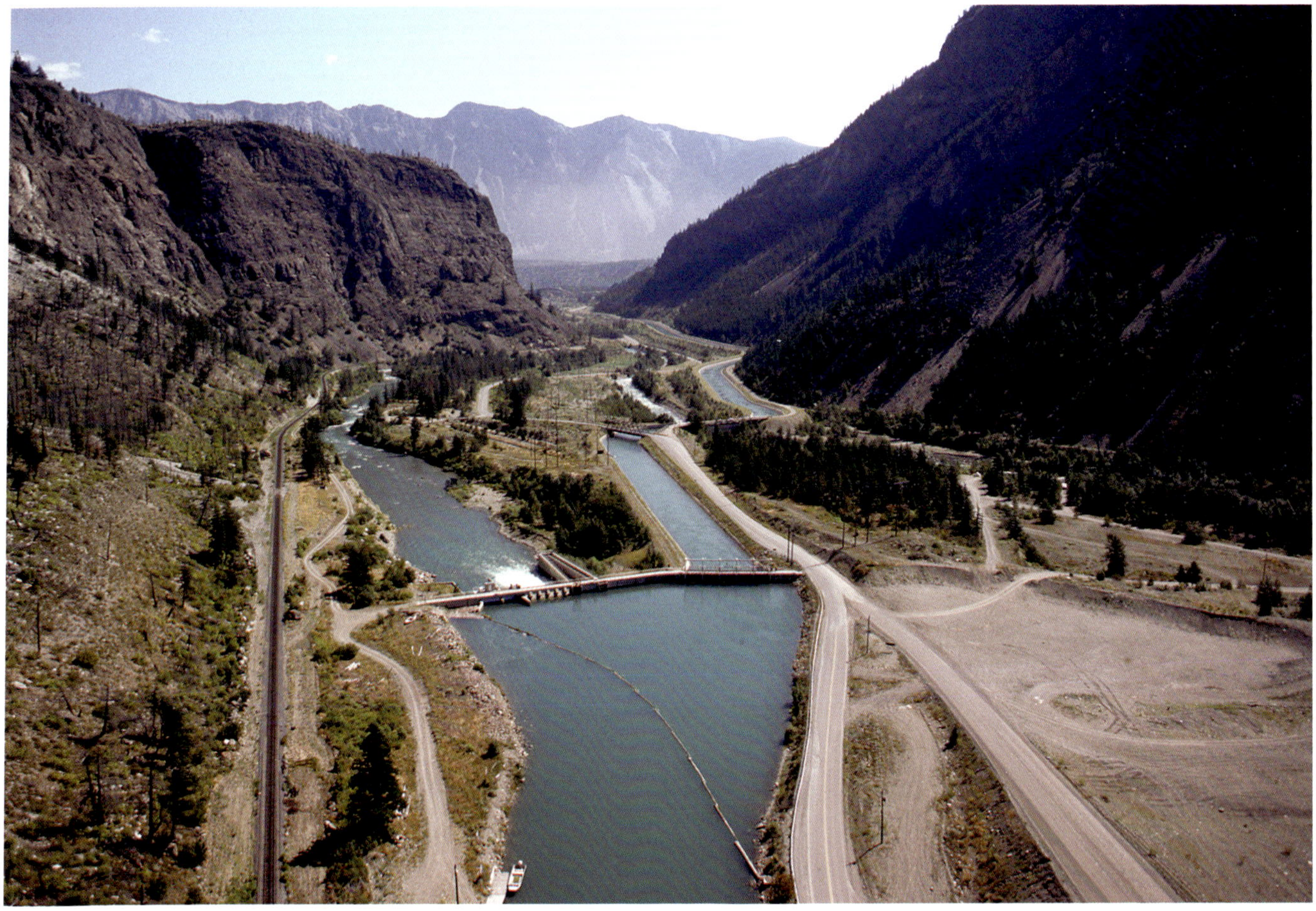

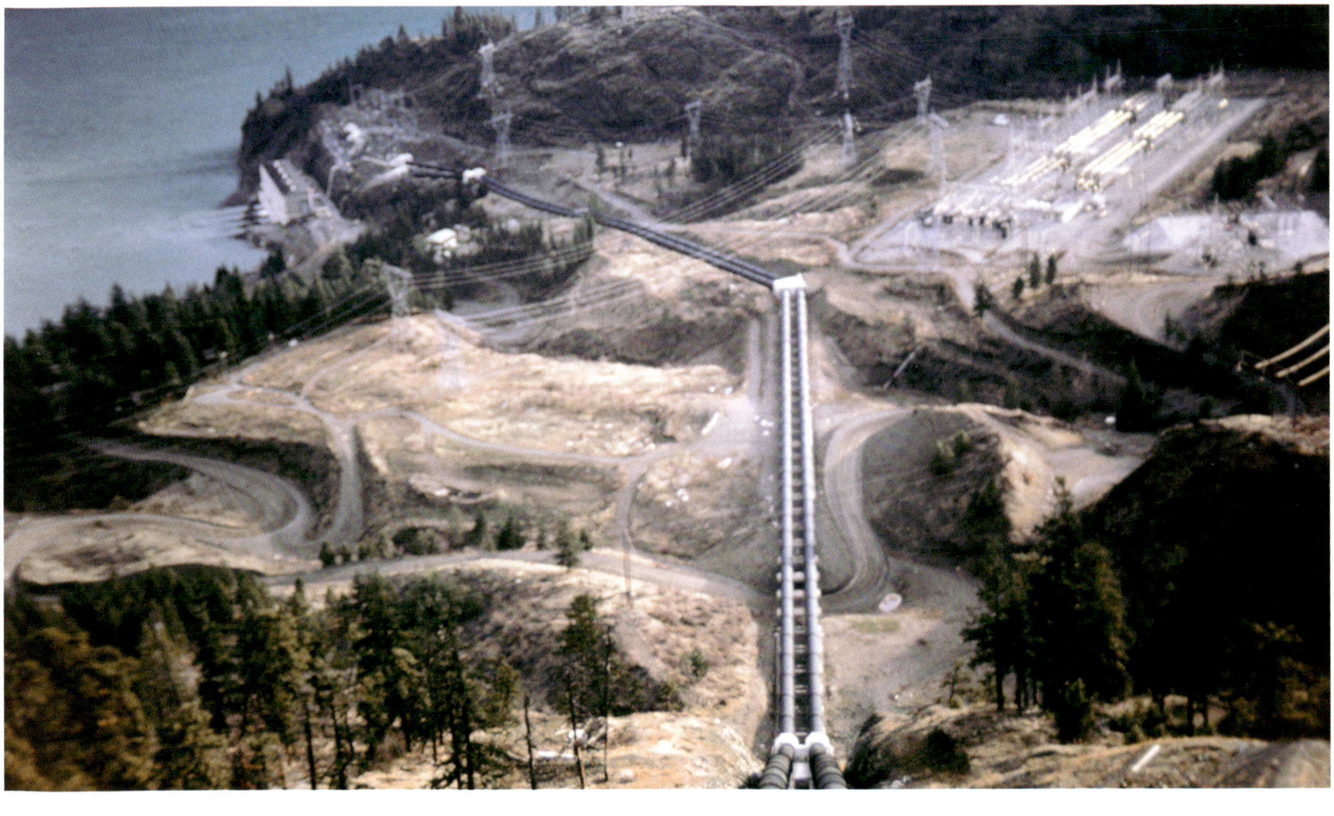

Grauer vs. Bennett

As the 1950s closed, economic development was gaining momentum in BC's north. That growth brought Dal Grauer his biggest challenge, from Premier W.A.C. Bennett, who wanted to dam the Peace River rather than rely on power supplied from the Columbia River Treaty Agreement between the US and Canada.

Bennett was a formidable advocate for the development of public power and had been the Canadian force behind the Columbia River Treaty. For several years, the Canadian and US governments had talked about developing a joint agreement to develop dams in the Columbia River basin, not just for power, but also to control flooding in the US as well as the Kootenays region of southeastern BC. Bennett had also created a "Two Rivers Policy" that saw hydroelectric development on the Peace River and the Columbia River, to open the northern region to opportunities and to provide power throughout BC. But in the 1950s, the province didn't have the funds necessary to bring the policy to life. The province would have had to purchase the rights to develop the Peace River for power, minerals, and pulp and paper from a wealthy Swedish entrepreneur named Axel Wenner-Gren, who owned them at the time.

As chief of the privately owned BC Electric, Dal Grauer refused to pay for hydroelectric development on the two rivers. It might have made sense to the premier, who wanted to grow the economy and the population, but Grauer had to answer to his shareholders. As well, he had the coal deposits of Hat Creek to develop for electricity to meet BCE's future power needs. Until the end, when he was sick in bed with leukemia, Grauer refused to relinquish control of the utility. On August 1, 1961, soon after Grauer died, Bennett's government passed a bill that called for the expropriation of BCE and changed the private company to the Crown corporation that is the BC Hydro and Power Authority.

BC Hydro would consist of BC Electric, the Peace River Power Development Company and the BC Power Commission. In the process, the new organization had acquired the rights and power development plans on the Peace River. The Power Commission had been established in 1945 to amalgamate power and generation facilities that were not served by BCE, and to extend service into un-serviced areas. With BC Hydro, Bennett would have a guaranteed market for the power his plants would produce. As well, he would be free to fund the dams and powerhouses on the Peace River at lower interest rates, reducing the project cost.

However, the government of the day had clearly been feeling a sense of grandeur and renewed vision for the future, and it was during the tenure of Premier W.A.C. Bennett that the company would finally meet its match. That day came on August 1, 1961, four days after chairman Dal Grauer died, at age fifty-five. It was the day of Grauer's funeral — held at Christ Church Cathedral in downtown Vancouver, just down the street from the BC Electric head office — that the BC government passed legislation allowing it to expropriate BCE and acquire it as a Crown corporation. The company would be amalgamated with the Power Commission. Former shareholders grudgingly accepted the $171,833,052 they were paid, after prolonged litigation. The takeover was not without controversy, and media at the time pitted business interests against those of the consumer. Respected business editor Harry Young of the *Victoria Daily Colonist* wrote that there was "little sign of mourning" that the Island would now be supplied electricity by BC Hydro.[18]

He also took issue with BC Power Corporation's belief that it had been paid an unfair price by the government. He argued that the price was in line with the market value of the stock. "Nor does it seem right that a company which for years has been given a non-competitive monopoly in the supply of energy and transportation over the most populous parts of BC should now expect the public to pay a fancy price, based on inflated values and on growth possibilities."

As a sign of the times, he defended "Mr. Bennett's bite into the private enterprise field," and wrote that "most of Canada is now receiving publicly-owned electricity on which the oppressive weight of the 50 per cent corporation tax does not have to be paid," referring to the savings for consumers who would no longer have to pay federal tax on their electricity.

Dr. Gordon Shrum became BC Hydro chairman; Hugh Keenleyside stepped down as chair of the Power Commission to become co-chair. The BCE building on Burrard was renamed the BC Hydro Building. In 1962, legislation was brought in that created the BC Hydro and Power Authority, which amalgamated the BCE and the Power Commission.

That year, work started on a new 260-mile (420-km), 230-kilovolt line from Bridge River to Prince George, along a route that had been reserved for the Peace River project. The Burrard Thermal plant was also scheduled to come into service that year, on the north shore of Burrard Inlet, 10 miles (16 km) east of Vancouver. It would serve the region while awaiting the power from the Columbia and Peace projects, which would, when built out, many times eclipse the Bridge River power project in terms of supply and magnitude.

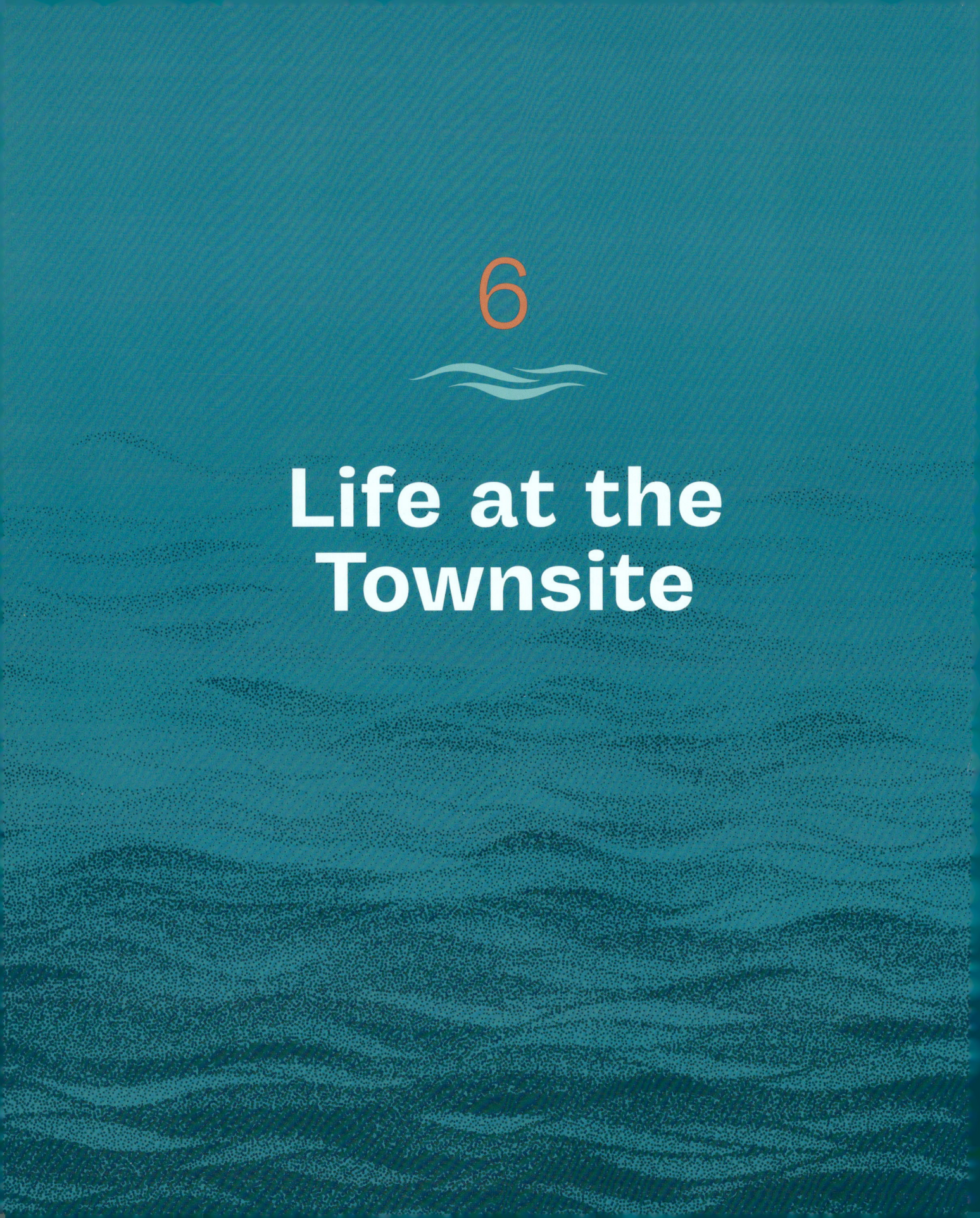

6

Life at the Townsite

The Bridge River community at Shalalth was always evolving as thousands of people over the decades passed through the makeshift town. With each phase of the development of the Bridge River hydro projects the town and the valley it occupied changed as well.

The fitful stop and start of the projects following the First World War, then through the Depression and the Second World War, caused an ebb and flow of construction workers and operations personnel. The end of the Second World War and the restart of the Bridge 1 and Bridge 2 projects, which were completed in 1960, defined another era. It created two communities: the construction camp and the company town set up to house the BCE employees who operated and maintained the facilities. But once the construction was complete, the camp shut down, leaving a relatively stable community that established its own identity in the valley for over fifteen years.

However, the digital age and the diminishing importance of Bridge River to the BC Hydro system — along with emergence of Hydro's own microwave telecommunication system, concurrent with the development of the large and remote hydroelectric projects on the Peace and Columbia Rivers — soon created opportunities for automation that would see the staffing strategy at Bridge River change completely. It was the end of an era for the Bridge River townsite and for the valley.

Before the Second World War

The purchase of the Bridge River Power Company by BCER in 1925 got the ball rolling with big plans to spend $30 million to develop the Bridge River system. One of the first jobs was to improve the narrow and twisting road between Seton Lake, the site for the generating stations, and the Bridge River Valley to facilitate the tunnel and dam construction. This necessitated a large townsite at Shalalth with a guesthouse, worker cottages, rows of family houses, a hospital, workshops, a community hall, a store, a schoolhouse, offices and bunkhouses. It even included a small branch office of the Canadian Imperial Bank of Commerce.

The Depression brought the activity to a halt in 1932, with the resulting reduction in staff to maintenance and security levels. However, in 1933 the price of gold soared in response to the collapse of markets, and the mines in the Bridge River Valley rushed to fill the demand. BCER responded by ramping up the installation of the decommissioned Unit 1 from Jordan River to service the growing mine load at the Bralorne mines.

The boom in Bralorne meant Shalalth became a hub of activity as workers and materials came in on the railway and were transported over Mission Mountain to the gold mines. Meanwhile, a temporary 24-inch (60-cm) penstock was constructed through the first 14-foot (4-metre) diameter tunnel completed through Mission Mountain in 1931.

The Jordan River unit was assembled, with all work completed in July of 1934 and the unit commissioned into service. BC Electric was then able to provide a strong electrical service to Bralorne and the surrounding mining communities.

The impact on the Bridge River townsite and surrounding community must have been significant. One minute the town and its services were overflowing with activity. The next it looked like a typical depression town. Then back again — all in a period of less than twenty-four months.

Dave Devitt was born in Bridge River. His family experienced early townsite life first-hand. Dave's dad, Jack, had started with BCER as a security guard at Buntzen around 1927. He was a bachelor at that time, but his "sweetheart" from school lived in the house next door in the Edmonds neighbourhood of Burnaby. BCER hired Jack at Buntzen for summer relief, to replace one of the two floormen who had gone on holiday.

He was then hired at Stave Falls for the summers until a full-time job came up at Buntzen. With a proper job, he proposed to his sweetheart and they got married and moved to Buntzen. She was not well, and Jack thought it would be good for her health to move to Bridge River, where the air is dry and the summer sun far more intense than it is on the coast.

These were heady times for the Devitts, who came to Bridge River in 1934 to start their family and a new job in the middle of the Depression. Once the construction was completed, the single unit powerhouse went into operation with a small complement of staff including Herbert Heinrich, a machinist from the Buntzen facility, who went on to operate/manage the plant. Later, his son John Heinrich, also a machinist who worked at Buntzen, would become area superintendent. He followed superintendent Chester Hunt, who died following a switching accident in the Bridge 1 switchyard in 1960.

The Second World War Era

At the outbreak of war with the Japanese in 1941 the BC Security Commission was looking around for places to relocate Japanese Canadians away from coastal communities. They were aware of the underutilized facilities at Bridge River. The shortages of manpower, materials and capital during the war had slowed the pace of development of Bridge River to a crawl. BCER president W.G. Murrin made the vacant townsite available to the commission for $15,000 a year. (See Chapter 4: Bridge River Internment Camp.)

Altogether about forty Japanese families lived in Bridge River alongside the BCER operating staff, including the Devitt family. The Japanese families set about doing their best in the new surroundings, including setting up their own school for grades one to eight. Although they didn't have a lot of money, they were industrious, creating their own community and setting off a bit of a boom for local and Lillooet businesses. Once again Bridge River was a functioning community.

FACING The Bridge River townsite in the late 1930s. Courtesy of the Jewish Museum

ABOVE Dave Devitt at two and a half years old at the summer house across Seton Lake from Bridge River. His father worked for the BCER and built the house. Courtesy of Dave Devitt

After the Second World War

The lack of progress on increasing the electrical supply to the Lower Mainland was catching up to BCE and they were facing a backlash in favour of public ownership of private utilities in the province. Dal Grauer had taken over from the retiring W.G. Murrin in 1946 with a promise to deliver $50 million in infrastructure, starting with Bridge River. With only the concrete-lined tunnel, completed back in 1931, BCE embarked on a program to compress the Bridge River project into four years. This conveniently coincided with the departure of the Japanese internees from Bridge after the war as the town was about to be transformed once again. In the British Columbia of the late 1940s and 1950s, it would have seemed like everybody in the province was either planning to work at Bridge River, or they knew someone who was.

During the construction of the late 1940s, there were about 500 men living in tarpaper shacks to the east of the family-oriented townsite. At the bottom of the hill was a blacksmith shop, so the hill was called Blacksmith Hill. The police officer lived at the top of the hill in a one-bedroom shack with a kitchen. The workers flocked to Bridge River for the jobs, fresh off war service and eager to start families and save up some money. Some loved the place, especially if they were happiest in the woods or on the water. A few bought properties and stayed or returned for the summers. It was even a vacation place, drawing adventurous people from the Lower Mainland for scenic picnics and fishing expeditions.

Once again the townsite changed to accommodate its new citizens. As Bridge 1 generating station took shape with the first unit coming on line in 1948, there was a need to operate and maintain the new facilities. The townsite morphed once again into a company town where BCE provided for the roads, the school, the houses and the community hall, and the company superintendent was the quasi mayor. It was a pretty idyllic life for a kid, with summers spent lakeside, or on a pair of water skis, and winters tobogganing down steep hillsides that no city kid would ever encounter.

According to Dave Devitt and his brother Phil, the original Bridge River school was in the townsite at the beginning of construction. It was moved to a new site flattened with fill from construction excavation to provide a ball field. Dave's brother Dean got a job lighting the furnace every morning at the new location. In the spring, the students would line up with rakes to clean the rocks off the playing field.

As Dave Devitt recounts, "everybody who lived at Bridge during the construction period recalls the same memories." Friday night was movie night, and a volunteer projectionist would load up a western that was shipped up on the

Budd Car from Vancouver. Kids and adults would cram into the community hall, shoulder to shoulder, for screenings of classics like *Stagecoach, Duel in the Sun, Destry Rides Again, Red River, The Gunfighter* — popcorn spilling as they cheered for the "good guys." On Saturdays, someone had the job of sending the film back to the city on the Budd Car. Otherwise, the kids spent their childhoods mostly outside, their parents having the advantage of knowing every single person in town. The semi-arid climate was ideal for gardening, and kids could pull carrots out of the ground, eat Bing and Queen Anne cherries, bright red and yellow, as well as apples straight from the trees in the orchards. "Everyone looked out for everyone. And everyone knew everything there was to know about everyone," says Devitt.

At Christmas, BCE would buy toys for the kids: trucks for the boys and dolls for the girls. The superintendent's wife or one of the teachers would mount a Christmas play, held in the community hall.

Life in Bridge River presented a few challenges as well. There wasn't much for grocery or other retail outlets in Bridge, so people had to come up with novel solutions. The teeth-clenching hour-and-a-half trek over Mission Mountain and the tough and expensive Moha Trail portion of the road to Lillooet would not be built until 1953. So, you could go to Lillooet by PGE gas car to

TOP The Bridge River school at its new location near the bottom of the Mission Hill Road. Courtesy of Mike Cleven, photographer unknown

BOTTOM The Bridge River tennis club with the guest house in the background. Courtesy of the Royal BC Museum

shop or you could order your groceries from the Woodward's department store in Vancouver or Yada's general store in Lillooet and pick up the order at the train station at Shalalth.

The men in the bunkhouses who worked at the dam sites were living a very different experience. Also, they'd often work round-the-clock shifts to get the work done. Malcolm Parry, who later made a name for himself as the *Vancouver Sun* society columnist, was twenty-one years old when he was hired at Bridge River. He says he was thrilled to have a room to himself. The bunkhouses had a bull cook who'd make the beds, and the cook banged on a triangle made out of a crowbar to summon them for meals. In summer, it would get up to 108°F (42°C), so there was a salt pill dispenser at the entrance to the mess hall.

They sat at long benches, and the mess hall served up heaps of eggs, bacon and pancakes flowing with syrup at breakfast, and giant beef roasts and T-bone steaks for dinner. There was also a cold buffet loaded with chicken, cold cuts, buns, pies and pastries. After their meals, the men would head to the camp commissary, where they'd snack on ice cream and candy, smoke cigarettes, and chat.

In 1952, the Devitts moved away to Ruskin after eighteen years in Bridge, to pursue opportunities at the Ruskin Dam and powerhouse, another generation project under development by BCE in the Fraser Valley.

As BCE grew and took over other companies, more people arrived in town. A year after the Devitts left for Ruskin, in 1953, a young electrician named Ben Hildebrand arrived to take one of the two floorman positions available at Bridge 1. Ben, who later retired to Kamloops, got his start with the company when it bought out the private power and water service he was working for in Ashcroft. The Ashcroft company had two or three employees and two small hydro plants, plus two diesel plants. Ben got the chance to do everything there, from digging ditches for water pipes to line work.

Once BCE purchased the Ashcroft water and power system, there was no longer a job for him at Ashcroft, so Ben took a job as a floorman at Bridge. The floorman was the eyes and ears for the supervisory operator, who was confined to the control room. The duties involved patrolling to check on the condition of equipment in all parts of the plant, the associated switchyard and the plant surroundings. Ben didn't like the shift work, which required him working long nights. When a job for an electrician was posted in 1957 at Clowhom Falls in Sechelt — accessible only by boat — he jumped at the chance. At Clowhom, he'd get more opportunities and develop experience in construction and bringing new generators on line, as well as maintaining those generators. He returned to work on the installation of all four units at Bridge 2 from 1959 to 1961.

Ben says the contract the BC Electric had with the Bralorne and Pioneer Mines was that if they couldn't supply power, they'd have to pay the mines' losses. It meant power to Bralorne was a major priority, but in heavy snowfall it was almost impossible to keep the lines energized. Trees would load up with snow, fall over and take the lines out. Snow was too deep for BCE's vehicles to make it over the mountain, but they had two Norwegian crew members who were top-notch skiers. They'd patrol the power line from Bralorne to Bridge River on their skis, carrying saws, hatchets and axes in case they needed to chop up any trees. The snow days of the 1950s were far worse than anything today. Even when Ben later lived in Lillooet, he didn't see anything as severe as he'd seen in Bridge River. "You don't see that anymore, conditions like that, of the worst kind. That's a pretty steep mountain. It was impossible to hike, the snow was so deep."

Ben described the Bridge River lifeline to Vancouver, the PGE's Budd Car (nicknamed "Budd Wiser"). With his wife and kids, he'd take the Budd Car rail service to Squamish, where it ended, and from there they'd take a Union Steamship ferry to get to Vancouver, to do shopping in the city. They'd return to the Bridge townsite by ferry and Budd Car. The trip each way was the better part of a day, so it was not a trip embarked on lightly, especially if the whole family was along for the ride.

The late 1950s saw the substantial completion of the Bridge River projects, including Bridge 2 in 1960. With that the construction camp wound down and the Bridge River townsite moved to its next incarnation.

FACING The Pacific Great Eastern (PGE) Railway gas car, with a flat deck railcar in the back for transporting vehicles, passengers and supplies between Shalalth and Lillooet. This was the primary mode of transportation before the Moha Road was built between Mission Dam and Lillooet in 1953. Courtesy of J.M. Stewart

VOICES FROM BRIDGE RIVER

From 1960 to 1980

As the Bridge River townsite settled into an operating phase after years of start and stop construction, it was not without some turbulence. Soon after BC Electric completed Bridge 2 in 1960, the province's political landscape began to move.

On August 1, 1961, the BC government passed legislation allowing it to expropriate BC Electric and declare it a provincial Crown corporation. In 1962, legislation was brought in that created the BC Hydro and Power Authority, and amalgamated the BC Electric and the BC Power Commission as one Crown corporation.

In some ways the merger didn't change things much in Bridge River. The needs of the generating stations and the people who operated and maintained them didn't change. But everything around them did. With the creation of BC Hydro came the amalgamation of the BCE system and staff with the BC Power Commission. It was a massive undertaking to restructure two large organizations into one, but it also meant employees all over the system had access to many more job opportunities. This was a boon for the employees at remote locations and only exacerbated the staff turnover at a time when recruiting qualified personnel was already very challenging.

Don Swoboda was an engineer-in-training in Bridge River during the late fifties and then an assistant superintendent in the early sixties. He recalls frequent and sometimes exciting trips on the Mission Mountain and Moha Roads (when the PGE's gas car was not available) while supervising the diesel plants in Boston Bar, Lytton and Spences Bridge or to visit family and friends in Vancouver. Nodding off on the Moha was not an option!

Swoboda recalls the exhilaration of hiking atop Mission Mountain with Harry Purney and Bob Heinrich and gazing down into the valleys of the Fraser and Bridge Rivers and Seton Lake. He found water skiing on Seton Lake, where the greatest fear was getting dunked in the always frigid glacier-fed water, was another fun way to socialize on summer evenings and weekends.

FACING Water skiers on Seton Lake in front of the Bridge 1 generating station. Courtesy of Mike Cleven, photographer unknown

TOP RIGHT BC Hydro engineer-in-training Don Swoboda with Bridge River area superintendent John Heinrich in front of Don's home in Vancouver in July 1960. Courtesy of Don Swoboda

BOTTOM RIGHT Bob Heinrich and Harry Purney on Mission Mountain. Courtesy of Don Swoboda

John Heinrich and his wife Wally were memorable dinner hosts for small gatherings of friends such as the Purneys, the Holts and the Fonsecas, after which it was traditional to enjoy a good singalong with Wally on the keyboard.

Swoboda also vividly recalls the tennis matches with Bill Russell and brothers Bob and Jack Heinrich but only after spending a lot of work repairing and resurfacing the aging tennis court with hot tar and sand.

The Ross family lived in Burnaby and spent summers in rented cabins at Seton Portage while their father, Bert, worked for Hume & Rumble on Bridge 1, Bridge 2 and Bridge River Terminal (BRT) over the years, including 1949, 1954, 1956 and 1958. Their son Ken eventually worked on the project as well and recalls the townsite as a revolving door of workers. Ken spent three years at Stave Falls as an apprentice operator before moving to Bridge with his wife Holly, who was expecting their first child. There he started his family and his first journeyman position as a power plant operator.

"Just about everybody there was young," he adds. "Some people used it as a stepping stone to their next job and others raised their kids there." Activities included softball teams and tennis and various social clubs, and a projectionist club for movie night. "Everybody volunteered for something."

Holly Ross recalls going into Lillooet on the train to do her shopping. If she had a hair or doctor's appointment or something, she'd stop in and order her groceries at Yada's. Once the order was complete they'd drop them at the train station for the Budd Car to deliver them to her in Shalalth. It was a great service and much appreciated. What they couldn't get in town they'd order by phone, and the pages of the Sears and Eaton's catalogues were well worn and dog-eared.

Harvey Lavigne was one of those who took advantage of the amalgamation, arriving in Bridge River as an apprentice operator in 1964. Before that, he'd been working in Port Alberni on the line crew, for the BC Power Commission, starting in 1956. He left Bridge River for a couple of years to work at the Burrard Thermal plant in Port Moody, then returned as an electrical operator and stayed until 1974. He eventually became a supervisor and helped set up some of the automation that would replace the operators, ending the townsite way of life. Harvey and his wife Joyce stayed in the area after Harvey retired in 1988. They built a house in Seton Portage but were displaced by a debris torrent off the mountain. They had to disassemble their home and move it to Lillooet in 1991. Harvey has good memories of his time in Bridge. He loved to hike up into the alpine areas: "It's waist high in wildflowers growing all over the place."

John Heinrich, the Bridge River area superintendent, relaxes at home with his ukulele and mandolin. John's father, Herbert, was a machinist and then the supervisor who helped bring in, install and operate the old relocated Jordan River unit in the first BC Electric powerhouse at Bridge River, in about 1932. Courtesy of Don Swoboda

By the time Bridge River was in full operation with a full complement of staff there would be about forty families living in the townsite. The round-the-clock supervisory operations alone required six operators. The additional electrical servicemen, mechanics, telecontrol technicians, floormen, helpers and the management and clerical staff added up to about forty staff. The number could increase depending on the complement of apprentices and trainees in the mix. The Bridge 1 supervisory operator controlled the operations at Bridge 1, with the assistance of a floorman. He also controlled the remote generation facilities at Bridge 2, Seton and Lajoie, and the Bridge River Terminal (BRT) substation. While the operators and floormen were on shift twenty-four hours a day, seven days a week at Bridge 1, the other three generating facilities and BRT only had servicemen on duty on a shift basis, to conduct station checks and undertake various maintenance duties. These staffing levels went largely unchanged until digital supervisory and control equipment was later introduced.

The townsite became a relatively stable village for about fifteen years, into the early 1980s. That didn't mean it started out with much in the way of amenities, but people brought what talents they had to bring the community to life. Dennis De Yagher had begun working at Bridge River as an operator at Bridge 1 in 1964 and was there through the early 1970s. He eventually became a production supervisor, first at Burrard Thermal and then back in Bridge River. He stayed at the townsite for the remainder of his career, finishing his last five years as manager. Dennis and his wife Corinne managed the movies on Friday nights and Saturday mornings. They organized getting the films from Vancouver on the Budd Car and running the projectors.

Dennis Osborne was the subforeman telecontrol technician. He had joined the British army when he was fifteen and was posted in Egypt, Singapore and Germany. By the time he arrived in Canada he had a family, and he got a job with BC Hydro in the mid-1960s. Dennis and his wife Brenda bought a house in nearby Seton

Girl Guides and Junior Forest Wardens, which included children from the townsite as well as the Indigenous community. Many of the teenage boys and girls also participated in the local gymkhana club.

The winter of 1968 was one of the longest cold spells in memory. With the temperature dropping to −20°F (−30°C) and below, outside workers were limited in how long they could work outside: twenty minutes out, twenty minutes in to warm up. The fog poured off the lakes day and night for a few weeks, and some people drove to Mission Pass just to see the sun shine. The lake froze over and teenagers put on their ice skates and went all the way to Lillooet. One of the local St'át'imc elders, Patrick Oleman, recalled that Seton Lake had frozen over only twice in his lifetime.

That long winter inspired another mode of entertainment. What do you do with a road covered in snow with multiple switchbacks and a 3,000-foot (900-metre) drop? Bobsleds, of course. You'd think this was the purview of the kids, but it was the adults who spent weekends working on the perfect design and fabricating their machines in basements and shops.

ABOVE LEFT The BC Centennial in 1971 was an excuse for some serious re-enactments of days gone by. From left to right: Jim Gemmill, Edgar Olsen, Ross ("Stretch") Downey, Sue Gemmill, Bob Nelless and Jackie Atkins. Courtesy of Bob Nelless ABOVE RIGHT The Christmas dances were always a special occasion with an appearance by Santa and gifts. Ross Downey is Santa, presenting wife Vicki Downey with a gift. The elf assisting is Ken Hood, the school principal. Courtesy of Jim Gemmill FACING TOP View of a frozen Seton Lake looking toward Lillooet in the winter of 1968. Courtesy of Ross Downey FACING BOTTOM Ross Downey (*front*) and Bill McKay were tough competitors in the Mission Mountain bobsled races. Courtesy of Ross Downey

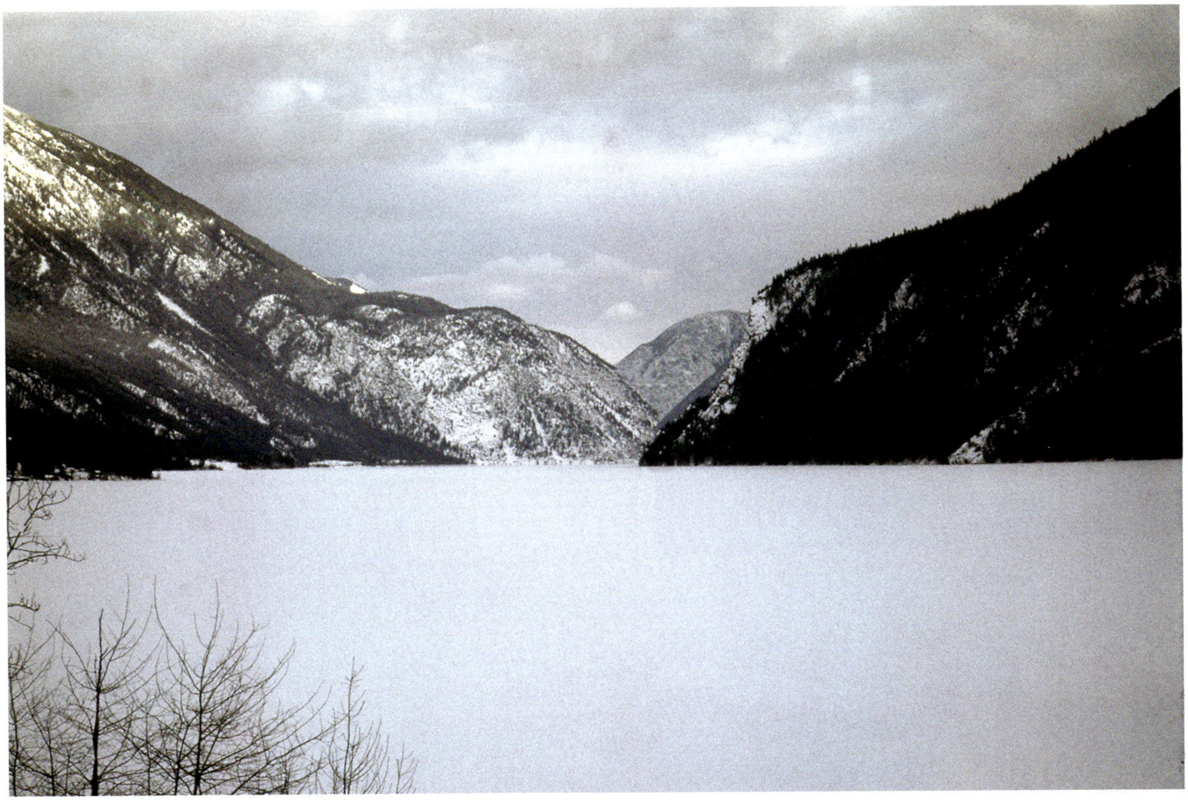

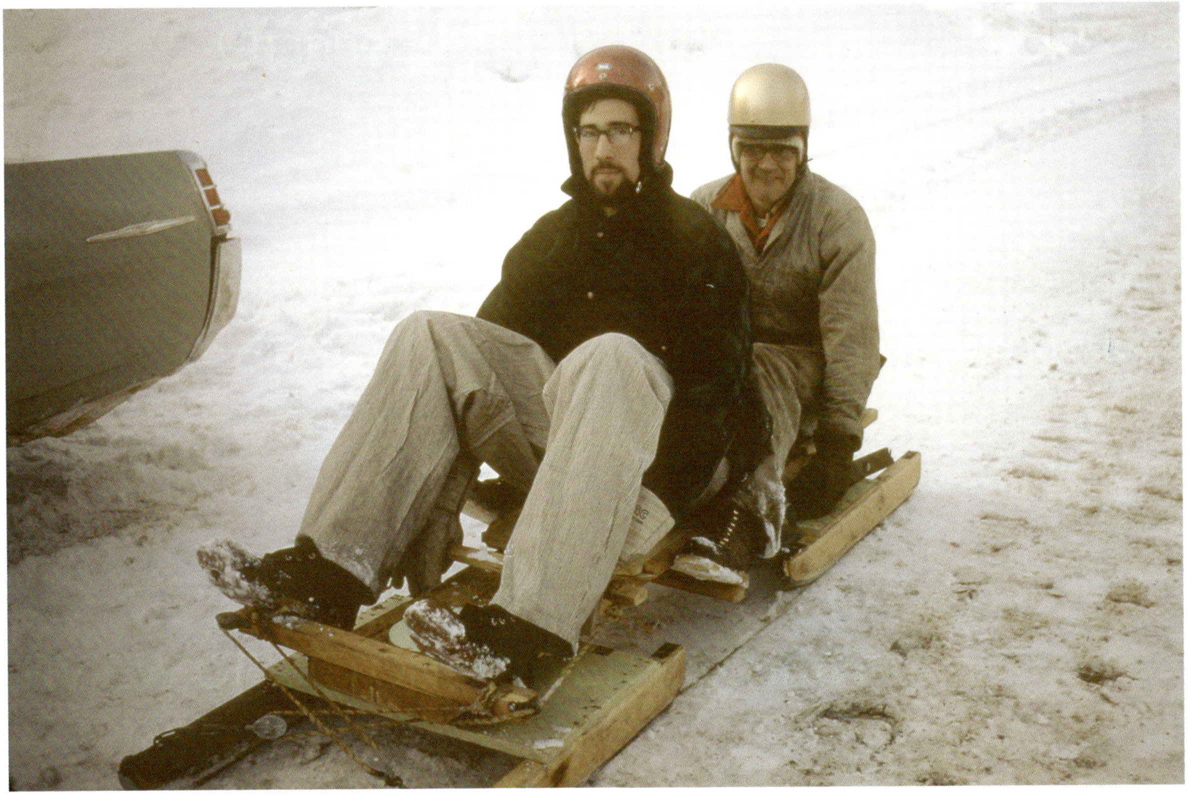

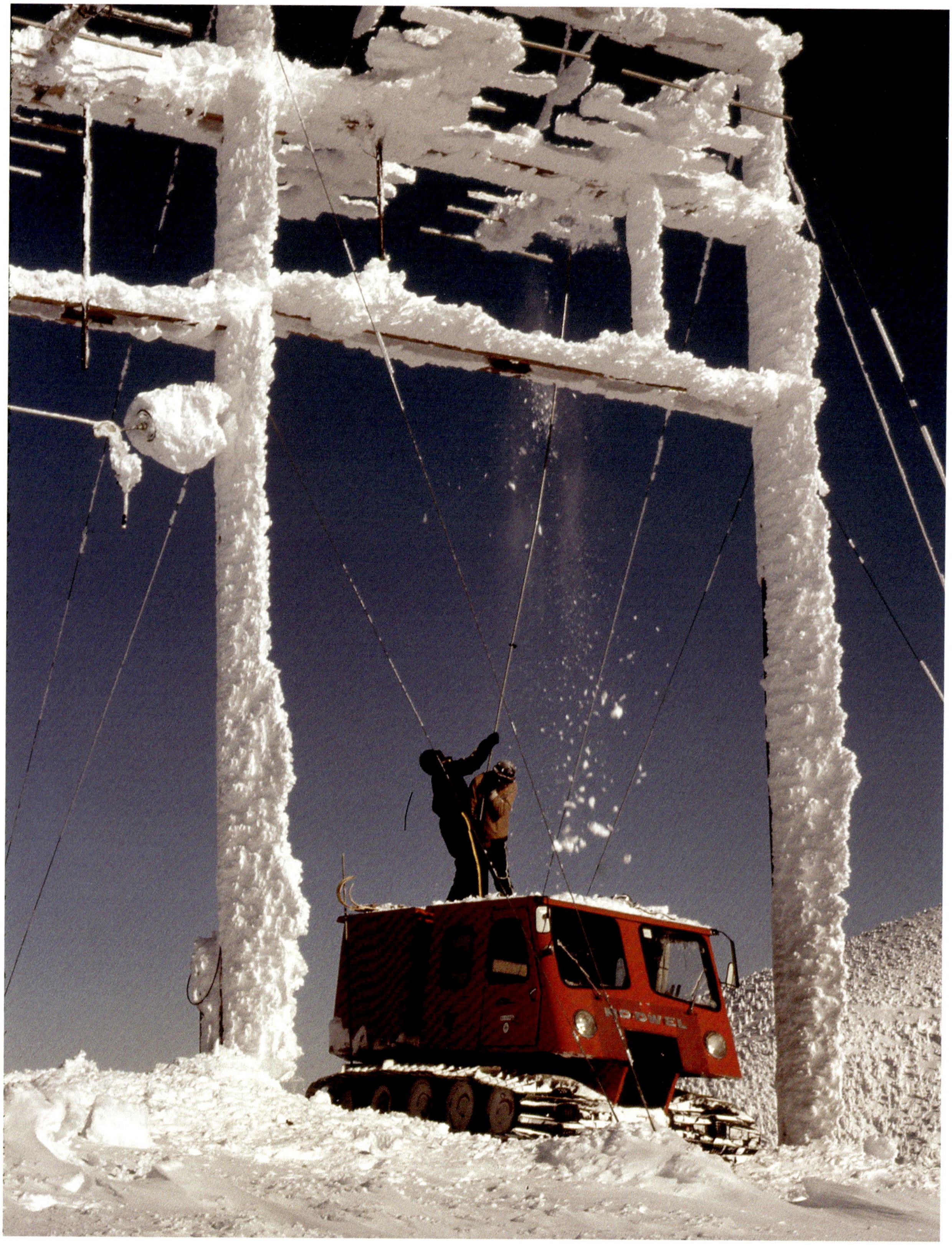

The cold weather helped vehicle tires adhere to the snow so Mission Mountain was not sanded much and the bobsled course was ready. After the first runs, and crashes, motorcycle helmets were worn by most of the sledders and brakes were added. Welding rods were tacked on to pipes that were inset in the bottom of the runners to keep the sleds from sliding off the road. After Seton Lake froze and the fog cleared, many runs were done at night. With the moon and stars reflecting off the snow, it was just like daylight. With two-way radios at the top and bottom of the hill to control traffic, the race was on for townsite bragging rights. The sleds were hauled on Walter Thompson's truck and the sledders by Bill McKay. At the bottom of the mountain much stomping of feet and jumping around was done to warm up. On race day, the school principal, Ken Hood, set up a 100-yard (90-metre) zone on one of the straightaways. Speeds of over 50 miles (80 km) per hour were clocked on that stretch. The five-and-a-half mile (9-km) course was completed in thirteen and a half minutes with an average speed of 25 miles (40 km) per hour. Not for the faint of heart! Over the six-week cold period the snow was measured in feet and parked cars in the townsite were marked with traffic cones on the roof to prevent being damaged by snow removal equipment.

FACING Dennis Osborne and an assistant clearing ice off the TV repeater antenna elements on top of Mission Mountain. Courtesy of Jim Gemmill

ABOVE Icing on the microwave antennae on Mission Mountain, where the cold interior air met the moist Pacific air from the coast. Courtesy of Jim Gemmill

Engineer-in-training Jim Gemmill and his wife Susan arrived in town in the summer of 1969. The couple settled into life in the community and made some lifelong friends with the other young couples living there. His initial focus was the microwave, VHF radio, supervisory and telecontrol work. He gives Dennis Osborne, the subforeman telecontrol technician, credit for mentoring him through a steep learning curve. In those years, Bridge River was a control hub responsible for monitoring Kelly Lake telecommunications and substation, as well as Bridge River Terminal and the Bridge 2, Seton and Lajoie plants.

Jim had been in a rock band in an earlier life, and as luck would have it an apprentice operator, Bob Nelless, and his wife Audrey moved to Bridge about the same time. Bob had also been in a rock band, so they teamed up with Ross Downey on drums and Jackie Atkins, the wife of an operator named Russ, on keyboard to form a band. The "keyboard" was actually an old church pump organ that had been sitting in the community hall, the kind that requires the player to pump foot pedals in order to generate the sound. They put a microphone inside its cabinet, and the notes groaned out so slowly, Jim says Jackie had to play three notes ahead of the band to stay in sync. But their covers of songs like "Proud Mary" and "Sittin' On the Dock of the Bay" were a big draw for the little community at the monthly dances.

At the time, the company was setting up a control centre on Burnaby Mountain, where they could manage all of BC Hydro's generation and transmission. "These were heady times," Jim recalls. "The Peace River was becoming the largest project on the system at the time and all communications between the Lower Mainland and the Peace River went through Mission Mountain microwave. Bridge River was in the midst of a major undertaking as we integrated our telecommunication systems with the new Burnaby Mountain control centre."

Schooling for the kids in Bridge River was a major challenge. It was not a location that many teachers aspired to. But those adventurous enough to come faced other challenges, especially if they were single. It was late on a weekend morning in late April 1967 when twenty-year-old Pat Wilson arrived on the PGE at Shalalth to begin her first teaching position.

Accompanying her was a classmate from UBC named Cathy, who was also up for an adventure in remote BC. They had boarded the train at eight a.m. in North Vancouver, with the two Bridge River Elementary School teachers they would be replacing, who would show them around the town. (The PGE rail line had been extended from Squamish to North Vancouver in 1956.) The Budd Car made its five-hour trip past Howe Sound and through Whistler and finally pulled into Shalalth.

Pat wrote down her initial impression: "I looked toward the town site. It was a strange scene of contrasts, as one side of the tracks was the beautiful milky green coloured lake and the picturesque mountains . . . and on the other side of the tracks there stood the town site and the penstocks on a bare hillside."

The "teacherage," where they'd live, was up the hill, away from the townsite, in a duplex with a furnished three-bedroom suite on one side, and a one-bedroom suite on the other. TV had not yet arrived in the valley. Their apartment had an old-fashioned phone on the wall with a separate earpiece. They were told they'd know if it was for them if the phone rang three times followed by a long ring. However, if it was three short rings only, then it would be a call for the chief who lived on the nearby reserve. She remembers the solitude of the place — but it wasn't serenity she felt, but a claustrophobic, hemmed-in feeling. It never quite went away.

"We would wait in hopeful anticipation for that long ring, praying that someone was contacting us from the outside world. Most often we were disappointed," recalls Pat.

They were in their early twenties and had hoped for more of a social scene in their time off. But most of the Hydro employees were married and many had kids. Watching the westerns on Fridays wasn't much of an option as the hall was mostly filled with kids who they taught during the day. Sometimes they'd be invited to someone's house for dinner, and she remembers one dinner where a small deer kept trying to eat off her plate. Her host, who worked for the PGE, had taken in a fawn whose mother had been killed on the track. There were other adjustments, too. One morning, she awoke with sawdust on her face because a pack rat was chewing a hole in her ceiling at the teacherage.

Ultimately, the remote location of the teacherage and safety concerns led to Pat and Cathy accepting an invitation from the Purneys to stay at their place for the balance of their time in Bridge. Notwithstanding some of the challenges Pat and Cathy faced, Pat has fond memories of her time with the kids and the Purneys as well as some lifelong friendships that were made there.

Pat and Cathy were in Bridge for two years at a time when the Indigenous schools and the provincial schools were separate, but in the late 1960s there were plans in progress to merge the schools. Barbara Simpson's parents had moved to Shalalth to run a store in 1964 while Barb was in university. After receiving her teaching degree at UBC in 1968, she took on her first position in Shalalth. The district superintendent and school principal would have been ecstatic that they were going to have some teacher stability in the elementary grades. It was an important time in the school system.

The federal and provincial governments had agreed to amalgamate the Indian Day School with the provincial elementary school for grades one, two and three. Jim Gemmill's wife Susan arrived with him in 1969 and was the grade one teacher. Barb had a grade two/three split and Clara Shields taught kindergarten.

However, this newly found teacher stability was not going to last. Harry Purney's son Rob was coming home from university to work in the summers. He met Barb at one of the monthly dances and soon they were married and off to pursue Rob's career. Jim and Susan had started their family and the school superintendent and principal were once again recruiting. But help was on the way . . .

Vicki Downey followed in Susan's footsteps by moving to the valley in 1970. She had graduated from UBC in 1969 and taught in Vancouver for a year before marrying Ross, who had been living and working in Bridge River since 1968, in July of 1970. The timing couldn't have been better with Susan expecting. Once again, the school district was delighted to hire someone who was coming to live in the valley. Vicki taught grade one in the same Indian Day School building as Barb and Susan now taught in, which in later years became the band office. "In those days, there were about six young couples, all our age, no kids," Vicki says. They never felt isolated.

Every day the train came through, and it could take them to North Vancouver, so it felt like a direct line to the city. They got news from afar, too: every morning, the train conductor would toss a stack of newspapers, tied up with string, at their train stop. It helped that Ross had travelled the Bridge River Valley since 1964. He went hunting there with his father, who was a lineman, and had worked on the power lines from Bridge River to Lillooet and over Mission Mountain from Bridge River to the Lajoie Dam. Because his dad knew everybody, they'd stay at the community hall in Gold Bridge on their hunting trips.

Ross and Vicki lived in one of the forty-four original townsite houses. In 1972, they moved back to the city so Ross could pursue his lineman apprenticeship after five years as a helper/driver and utilityman in Bridge River. Again, the district superintendent and principal Ken Hood were on the hunt for teachers.

The situation for the older kids, grades eight to twelve, was more complicated. There were no high school facilities in Bridge so the kids had to take the Budd Car to Lillooet on Sunday afternoon and stay in dormitories through the week, taking the Budd Car back home on Friday afternoon. It was a significant challenge for parents and kids alike. The situation persisted until about 1979 when production supervisor Dennis De Yagher, manager

Glen Finney and the local St'át'imc community petitioned the railway, by then called BC Rail, to look into better transportation for the students. With an agreement between Hydro, the local Tsal'alh (Seton Lake) Band and the Lillooet School Board, a self-powered passenger car was purchased from the eastern US and refurbished by BC Rail in Squamish so that the thirty-five students could travel to Lillooet each day in the morning, along part of the passenger car's route, returning home on the scheduled Budd Car leaving Lillooet about four-thirty in the afternoon. Later, BC Rail would replace the service running between Lillooet, Seton Portage and D'Arcy with a pair of railbuses. The service, which became known as the Kaoham Shuttle, still runs today and is managed by the Tsal'alh.

ABOVE BC Rail replaced the service between Lillooet and nearby Seton Portage and D'Arcy with a pair of railbuses, subsequently named the Kaoham Shuttle. Courtesy of Dave Devitt

The 1980s to . . .

The townsite entered its next, and final, transition phase during Dennis De Yagher's tenure as production supervisor.

It was inevitable that the townsite would be wound down, Dennis says. "The interruption of the output of all the generation facilities in Bridge River wouldn't add up to the output of two of the ten units at the Bennett Dam." New digital technology allowed close monitoring of the generation and transmission facilities and automation allowed all aspects of operation to be carried out from centralized facilities in Langley, with Vernon serving as a full-capability backup control centre. This development, along with the very real difficulties of retaining staff in the area, even with the improved school arrangements for the older students, made maintaining a full townsite impossible to justify. Operators were the first to go in the mid-1970s, followed by the maintenance people over time as staffing levels were reduced through attrition. Eventually, the houses were used only for itinerant staff who travelled into Bridge River from their homes for four days in and three days out. The houses were eventually replaced by modern fourplexes.

Dennis and his wife Corinne had grown so fond of the place they bought a house overlooking Anderson Lake. He says that when the powerhouses became automated it was a major transformation — not just physically, but culturally — for the whole valley. "It radically changed the community because it went from a community where families lived, with all their spouses and kids, to an employee-oriented situation."

Today the townsite, which housed up to forty BC Hydro families at its peak, is silent. Little can be seen of the incredible past of that amazing place. You'd think you could hear the reverberation of a community where so many people came to make their way over the better part of a century. A few new fourplex buildings remain for the use of the operating and maintenance staff who commute to the site weekly. With the completion of the Bridge 1 and 2 generator replacements and the La Joie Dam upgrade, there will be little left of the original townsite other than the memories of all the people who lived there over the ages. Except, perhaps, for the miniature castle, with windows made out of the glass from antiseptic bottles, built by Dr. Fujiwara and his son Alan. The valley has been changed forever, but, with the completion of the work, you may once again be able to hear the grasshoppers on a hot summer day.

FACING By the early 1980s the staff at Bridge River had been significantly reduced. Staff worked on rotation and were housed in new fourplexes that replaced the earlier detached houses at the townsite. Courtesy of BC Hydro Library and Archives, photo by Jim Shepherd

ABOVE Dennis and Corinne De Yagher at their Seton Portage home overlooking Anderson Lake. They spend their summers in Seton Portage and winters in Vernon. Courtesy of Dennis and Corinne De Yagher

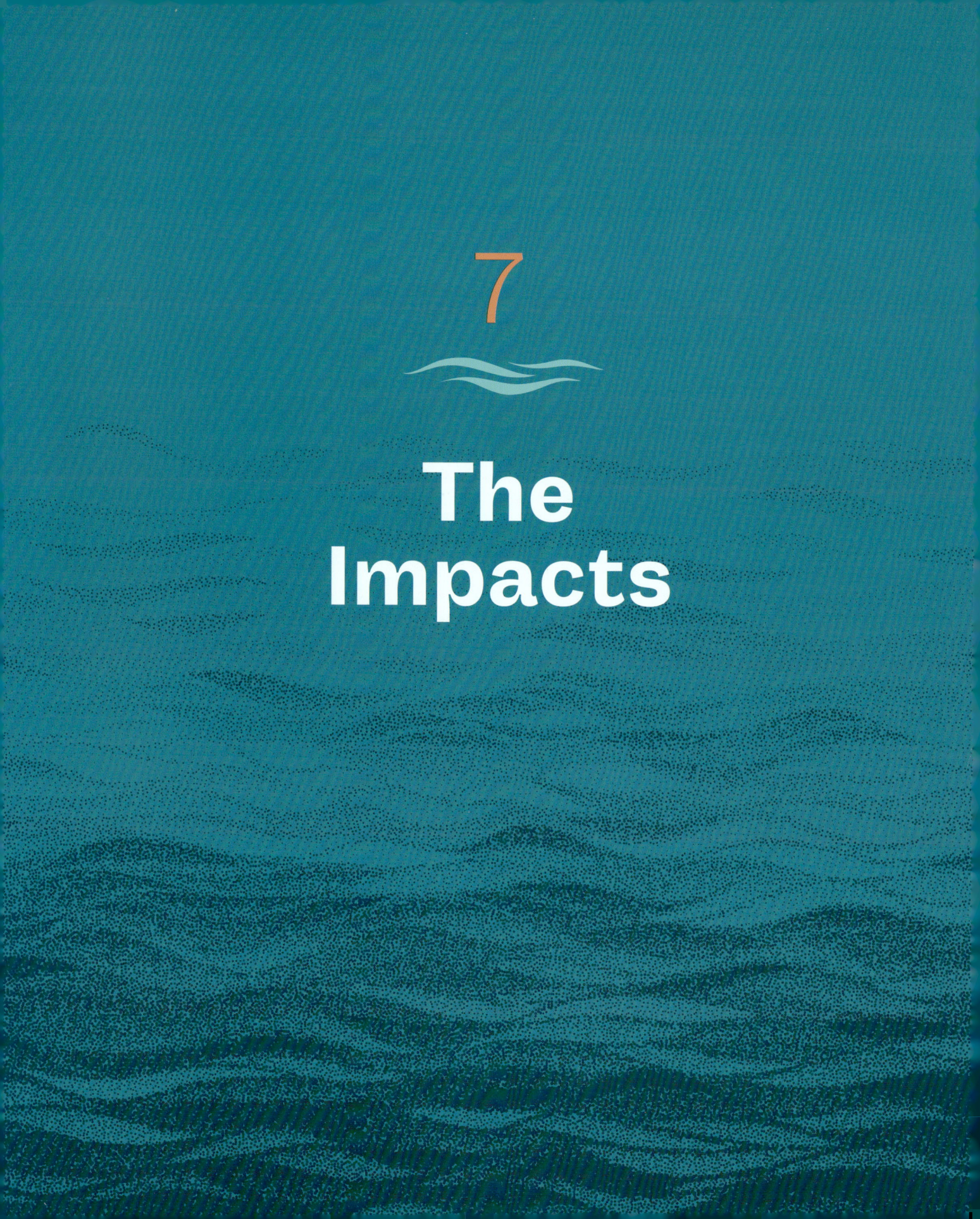

7

The Impacts

The hydro project was a major achievement, and a testament to human ingenuity, but there were costs, too. When BCE built Mission Dam and created the reservoir that would become Carpenter Lake, it flooded a major road, several ranches, a small town and two settlements in the process. Carpenter Lake is about 30 miles (50 km) long, or twice the length of Vancouver's Burrard Inlet, and it now occupies the space of the flat-bottomed upper Bridge River Valley, which had been rich with game and fish.

The original road that ran alongside the river had been used for years to connect people from Bralorne to Shalalth. It was to be flooded, and a new road much higher along the reservoir had to be built. Also, the 60-kilovolt transmission line, built in the early 1930s, had to be relocated to higher ground. The reservoir filled faster than planned, and there was some concern that one of the bridges on the road might not get built in time. Fortunately, the bridge was finished and the new road opened before the old road was flooded out.

The first settlement to be flooded was Rexmount, in 1958. It was about 12 miles (20 km) up the Carpenter Lake Reservoir from Terzaghi Dam, just east of the Jones Creek junction, with a population of about 200 people at its peak. BC Directories lists about two dozen families living at Rexmount at the time, as well as a store, two roadhouses (hotels), livery stables, a blacksmith shop, a garage, a post office, and several ranches, orchards and market garden stalls along the road. The settlement served the local miners and prospectors in the surrounding area, many of whom had come to find gold but had decided to lay down roots instead.

In late 1959, two more settlements were flooded, Wayside and Congress, which were little more than a scattering of cabins and bunkhouses. The bigger town to be flooded was the company gold mining town of Minto City, which is now in the upper reaches of the lake, in the mudflats. From 1942 to 1945, it had been used as an internment camp for Japanese Canadians.

Minto Gold Mines had begun operation in 1933, the third-largest producer of gold in Bridge River Valley, with iconic character Big Bill Davidson as president. Davidson was also one of the founding fathers of Minto City and was so determined to make it a destination that he even cleared land for a rodeo grounds, which was pretty exciting for the valley at the time, with pavilions, dances and prize money. But once the gold vein ran out and the mine closed, the bustling little town became sleepyville. By then, Big Bill Davidson had died, so he never did see his town flooded. Prospector and BCER surveyor Mel Stewart remembers visiting Davidson in his dying days. "The last time I saw Big Bill he was ill. He was lying on his big old chesterfield with the fancy back to it, and he had a big rug over him. He didn't get up. I forget why I went to see him, something to do with the work I was doing. But that was the last I saw of him. I gather he died in Bralorne's hospital."

Today, when water levels are low, imprints of building foundations and roads can still be made out beneath the water at the western end of Carpenter Lake.

Charlie Cunningham, who'd lived in the Bridge River Valley since 1933, was hired by BCER to buy up the land that was to be flooded. He was also assigned the task of removing anything of value before the flooding. Cunningham had been a big game guide and wildlife photographer prior to his work with BCER, which took him to Vancouver for two years to work at the BC Electric office. He then worked on the Peace River project, negotiating the purchase of lands prior to the dam being built at Portage Mountain.[1]

VOICES FROM BRIDGE RIVER

Construction superintendent Andy Cleven's family left the BCE townsite in 1962, after the work was completed, when son Mike was seven years old. Mike remembers what it was like visiting local residents with his father, before the valley was flooded:

Dad was friends with many of the men who lived and worked along this road, and because of his p.r. skills was something of a liaison with the ranchers, trappers, settlers, prospectors and others who'd made it their home. I remember being taken into old log cabins on his visits to them, full of wood smoke and stranger smells — furs and hides, curing meat, strong drink and stronger tobacco, the smell of wet — or just old — clothes and other bits of memory that are hard to define and sort out now. Shaggy old men in tiny cabins whose lives were something out of the nineteenth century, who had struggled with this incredible wilderness in their time and in it found a special place like no other.[2]

FACING View from the Lajoie dam at the Bridge River headwaters with the Hurley River on the right and Mount Truax in the background. Photo by Don Swoboda

Reservoir Cleanup

Before the flooding of the valley, there was no cleanup effort to remove the trees and debris. Carpenter Lake was an unsightly mess, with floating wood debris piled up in huge booms to be kept away from the dam and spillways. But it was visible from the road that ran along the lake. Eventually the company decided that if they had to go to so much trouble controlling the mess, they might as well get rid of it entirely.

In 1970, BC Hydro launched a major cleanup program to clear out 1,200 acres (490 hectares) of dead trees and wood debris. Because Carpenter Lake is fully drawn down every five years before the spring runoff, it enabled the BC Hydro engineers to inspect the dam. The deep drawdown year also allowed locally hired workers and the company's construction crew to go in and clear out the dead trees that were still standing in the lake. About thirty men and six bulldozers tore down trees and stacked them and other debris into huge piles for burning. They had a small window of time to finish the work. Once the spring runoff began again, the crews had to retreat. They used boom boats to gather up any floating debris and towed it to shallow areas to be stored until the water naturally dropped again in the following year, when it would be piled up and burned.

VOICES FROM BRIDGE RIVER

But by 1976 that gather-and-burn strategy was stopped, because it was too costly to cut down trees, gather the logs in shallow areas, pile them and burn the pile once the water had retreated and the weather had dried them out. By that time, it was also too risky to start a fire, what with the potential for starting a forest fire. The company found a local entrepreneur to gather the wood and salvage it instead of burning it, a win-win for both company and entrepreneur. Because BC Hydro didn't have the high cost of removing the wood, it didn't get transferred to consumer electricity bills. And it created a few new jobs in the area.

The entrepreneur, Paul Polischuk of Lillooet, was contracted to truck the cottonwood from Carpenter Lake to a New Westminster pulp and paper mill. He sold fir logs to a Lytton sawmill.

Business was brisk enough that he had plans to start a second sawmill producing cottonwood veneers for the US plywood industry.

"Hydro has a big problem removing debris from lakes, especially on the older projects built when the obligations to log the land weren't very clear," said Fraser Valley production department manager Peter Tattersall, in an edition of the company's *Intercom* newsletter, in 1977. Another key consideration was the lack of available sawmills or pulp mills to process the high volumes of fibre, notes Don Swoboda.

Surveyor Mel Stewart put in a bid to clear and salvage the debris. He says there wasn't a lot of good timber on the valley floor but there were a lot of aspen poplars. Once the valley was flooded, the trees died and many of them floated to the surface. The company had to contain them in a catchment area to keep them from pounding against the dam and damaging it. "It was a bloody mess," he recalls. "So much debris, you could walk across the logs from one side to the other." He didn't get the job, but his plan had been to start a portable sawmill for wood chipping. By this time, the road to Lillooet had been completed (in 1954), making access to markets more viable.

FACING View of Carpenter Lake looking upstream from the Terzaghi Dam circa 1970. Courtesy of Jim Gemmill

Impact on Fish Stocks

One of the biggest challenges in the development of hydroelectricity is the impact it has on the natural environment when reservoirs are created, particularly to fish stocks. In the early years of Bridge River, such protection wasn't a top priority. However, by the 1950s there was an awareness that the fishing industry could be compromised, and a fish ladder was included in the construction of the Seton Dam at Lillooet. Prior to the project, sockeye and pink salmon stocks had been rebounding decades after the devastating blow to fish stocks from the Hell's Gate landslide of 1913. After the disaster, there were no pink salmon reported at their natural spawning grounds in Seton River, or Portage or Cayoosh Creeks, until 1945, after a fish ladder was installed at Hell's Gate. Prior to the Hell's Gate landslide, there were a reported 200,000 pink salmon that had spawned at Seton River. Fisheries authorities recognized that this was a vulnerable spawning ground in need of protection.

An agreement had been made between BCE and several fisheries agencies in 1953, the same year construction had started. The plan was to protect the trout and salmon stocks once the Seton River project was complete, and BCE made efforts to protect the fish. The agreement — between BCE, the Canadian Department of Fisheries, the BC Game Commission and the

FACING Pink salmon returning to spawn in the Upper Seton Spawning Channel. Courtesy of Splitrock Environmental Sekw'el'was LP

International Pacific Salmon Fisheries Commission—settled on the need for a fish ladder to allow fish to pass upstream over the dam and onwards to Seton and Anderson Lakes. In addition, a screen was installed to prevent adult fish from being swept down the canal to the powerhouse.

During construction, the creek was not to be diverted until the pink salmon fry had made their journey to the ocean. However, the company also knew from studies that about 10 percent of sockeye salmon smolts would be killed due to the construction, despite their best efforts.[3] It was also acknowledged that the spawning ground for pink salmon above the dam site would be seriously impacted by the change in water depth and velocity.[4] As well, for the fry that did emerge, many wouldn't survive the journey through the turbine or find safe passage down the dam's fish ladder. A 1958 study by International Pacific Salmon Fisheries commissioners F.J. Andrew and G.H. Geen concluded that both pink and sockeye stocks were reduced due to the diversion of Bridge River water to Seton Lake.

Salmon survival had become an issue. The company, still privately owned, had been considering the Moran Canyon on the Fraser River as the next obvious site in hydro development, but also acknowledged that the river was a major destination for significant salmon runs.

The Fraser might have harnessed a terrific amount of energy, and been close to urban areas and therefore economical, but the threat to fish stocks was simply too high. Instead, the company set its sights on the Peace River, which was within the Canadian boundary, and the Columbia River, which required an agreement with the US, since it was an international river. The Peace River had no salmon stocks, and the Columbia River's stocks had already dramatically dropped because of dam projects built in the US in the 1930s, particularly the Grand Coulee Dam. The company had also purchased the Hat Creek Coal deposits, which gave them a thermal power option.

BCE incorporated the Peace River Power Development Company to study the transmission of power to the Lower Mainland. They'd hoped to bring power from the Peace and Columbia by the mid-1960s, but of course the company would be expropriated by 1961 and the project would be taken over by the province. By that time, Premier W.A.C. Bennett had devised the "Two Rivers Policy." That policy was to focus on power development on the Peace River, and build three storage dams on the Columbia's Canadian side as part of a treaty agreement with the US. He planned to sell Canada's 50 percent share of the additional power generated by existing American dams built on the Columbia decades ago, and use the funds for the construction of generation at the Mica Dam.

Bennett knew better than to look to the Fraser for development. "He knew there was political heat on the coast for protecting the salmon on the Fraser," says UBC professor Matthew Evenden. "There was the canning industry, a range of civic groups who supported the idea of protecting salmon, early conservation, and different First Nations in creating an alliance against dam development on the Fraser." The BCE spent a lot of money studying whether salmon could survive Fraser River development, but if American dams were any guide, it was highly

VOICES FROM BRIDGE RIVER

ABOVE An unidentified fisheries technologist (*left*) with fisheries technicians Brian Frank and Pricilla Frank, both members of the Sekw'el'was (Cayoose Creek) Band, using an electrofisher to conduct sampling of out-migrating salmon smolts in the Lower Seton Spawning Channel. Courtesy of Mike Flynn, Department of Fisheries, photographer unknown

FACING Splitrock Environmental's Remmy Dillon, a fisheries technician and member of the Sekw'el'was (Cayoose Creek) Band, using a fish viewer to magnify and identify a pink salmon smolt in the Lower Seton Spawning Channel. Courtesy of Splitrock Environmental Sekw'el'was LP, photograph by Kathleen Street, Senior Fisheries Technician

risky. And there was a Pacific Salmon Treaty that protected American sockeye and pink salmon stocks, which also impacted the debate.

In 1961, the first artificial spawning channel was constructed to accommodate up to 7,000 returning pink salmon. This upper channel was located beside the Seton River just below the dam, and replaced the original spawning habitat flooded out due to the elevation of the Seton Dam.

Additionally, approximately 30,000 square yards (25,000 square metres) of pink salmon spawning habitat in the Seton River was lost by the diversion of flow away from the river and into the canal to the powerhouse, then into the Fraser River once discharged from the Seton generating station.

The loss of pinks and sockeye had come to the attention of the Salmon Commission. To address the issue, the BCE donated land obtained through a lease agreement with what was then the Cayoose Indian Band for a project to replace lost river spawning habitat. Based on positive results from the 1961 test spawning channel, a two-mile (3-km) spawning channel, known as the lower channel, was completed in Seton River in 1967 to accommodate 20,000 spawning salmon.

In 2002, the lower spawning channel underwent a complete rebuild with major improvements in habitat complexing, renewed spawning gravels, natural rock placements and improved water flow management and operational facilities. Members of the Cayoose Band were directly involved in the reconstruction and the Sekw'el'was, as they are now known, are now responsible for the operation and care of these critical salmon restoration facilities.

Land Encroachment and Other Impacts

The other impacts to the St'át'imc were the expropriations that bisected and encroached on their reserve lands. (See Chapter 3: Valley of Plenty.) The project today is flanked on both sides by reserve lands. "What's unusual about the Bridge system is the Shalalth generating facilities and Seton Dam, canal and powerhouse are right there, right next door to the reserve lands — real neighbours," says BC Hydro president Chris O'Riley. "And if you look at the land there, part of the sensitivity of it is the valley is so steep, and you have a little bit of shore, so there was very little land to begin with, and when the company took a bunch of it, you can see the legacy of that."

The powerhouses at Shalalth are situated on former reserve land, as is the power canal at the other end of Seton Lake. The canal was built across the reserve property of an elder named Moses Frank. The transmission line that ran from the Bridge system south and through to Harrison Lake also cut across extensive reserve lands.

"If you look at the transmission lines that come through the territory, they hit all the reserves," says Rod Louie, former implementation manager for the St'át'imc Government Services. He says that between Hydro, the PGE and highways projects, the St'át'imc lost significant reserve land.

For decades, several St'át'imc communities had to put up with the huge transmission towers looming over their properties, but they didn't have access to the electricity the lines were carrying. Instead, they had diesel-run generators provided by the Department of Indian Affairs. The staking of a water licence on Tipella Creek, outside Port Douglas, by an independent power producer (IPP) in 2002, led eventually to the development of a small power plant and a transmission power line connection to the isolated St'át'imc communities.

And then there were the required spills that are part of the dam system. For several decades, excessive inflows and flooding required BC Hydro to make deliberate and controlled spills from the reservoirs, a practice that happened about every three years between 1960 and 1992. But in August 1991 an incident occurred that put BC Hydro on a path to a pioneering management program over the Bridge River watershed. There had been extreme rainfall in the late summer of 1991 that melted more glacier pack than usual. It was a rare event with drastic consequences. The reservoirs were full and Hydro personnel had to make the difficult decision to make emergency spills from the Terzaghi Dam. Without releasing the water, the structural integrity of the dam was in jeopardy. However, the torrential release of water would also wreak havoc to the riverbed and the downstream spawning grounds.

Electrical engineer Malcolm Stewart was about one month into his new job as area manager of the Kamloops hydro operations, which included Bridge River. The decision had been made to transfer the operating authority on the Carpenter Reservoir from Burnaby Mountain to the area manager. The rainfall that year had been at a level not seen for decades. The Carpenter Reservoir behind the Terzaghi Dam was rapidly rising, and the physical security of the dam was of imminent concern. "I can still remember standing on top of the dam in the pouring rain talking with the Department of Fisheries and Oceans and the Indigenous community, looking at the options," says Stewart. "It was a difficult choice. We certainly didn't want dam failure." It was a tough decision not only for environmental reasons, but also because the DFO enforcement officers were threatening charges if the spill resulted in any damage to the fish or their habitat, says Stewart. Although Hydro biologists were working on a plan with DFO biologists, ultimately, the outcome would fall on Hydro's shoulders. And because charges could be laid against an individual employee who was responsible for environmental damage, Stewart was concerned that charges could be levelled at him personally. There had already been a precedent-setting case, the Bata Shoe Company case, in which an employee who poured chemicals into a river had been charged, even though he was following his employer's direction. Stewart found himself between a rock and a hard place, and in an incredibly stressful situation. "I would say I lost most of my hair in those years," Stewart says.

Once the Terzaghi Dam was constructed, water flow to the Bridge River had been cut off. Any water flow was the result of natural spring flows and tributaries downstream of the dam. The DFO wanted a minimum flow restored from upstream behind the dam, believing that it would improve the fishery, says Stewart. Stewart's role was to coordinate with the DFO and all community members, including the St'át'imc Nation. He held community hall meetings where he faced many who were already angry with the construction of the dam and didn't welcome the idea of a release of dam water that would potentially damage more fish habitat or impact their communities. He coordinated the outcome with First Nations groups, government agencies and the Hydro control centre on Burnaby Mountain, who provided guidance on the volume of releases and any weather changes.

Electrical engineer Ralph Legge, whose career at BC Hydro spanned thirty-six years, worked at the control centre and was then responsible for operational coordination of the hydro projects on the BC Hydro system. "The study of weather systems is a huge part of the planning, operation and monitoring of a hydro project's operation, within its watershed and river system, and in coordination with other projects within their watersheds and river systems. There are so many pieces of a river system. It's a balancing act, and every year can be quite different," he says. "There was one year that even with all available information, planning and coordination possible, the Columbia River came within six inches of flooding the city of Portland, Oregon."

Stewart said he was Hydro's go-between for all impacted parties, who collectively agreed on a water release plan. "We tried as hard as we could," he says. "The best outcome would have been for the rain to stop and so no water would have to be released. I had never seen rain like that in my life. We made a herculean effort to manage the impact of the water release and to collectively meet everyone's expectations, especially the DFO. We were hoping that by agreeing to a plan, we would avoid charges."

Stewart executed the agreed-upon plan, knowing that he could only hope that it would result in the least damaging outcome. Before the first release, Hydro staff secured the area, to ensure that there would be no loss of life as a result of the water release.

Prior to Stewart's involvement, electrical engineer Wing Joe, who oversaw all generating systems from the control centre, had already determined that spills would be necessary. He knew from the March forecast that the snowpack runoff that fed into Carpenter Reservoir was higher than normal. There are only two ways to discharge water from the dam: running it through the generators or by spilling it out of the Terzaghi Dam. He had been running the Bridge River generators at full capacity of 5,400 cubic feet per second (CFS), or 150 cubic metres per second, in an effort to lower the Carpenter Reservoir as much as he could. Because the Seton generating station couldn't handle as much flow, he directed staff to spill continuously at Seton Dam to allow for the extra water flowing into Seton Lake from Carpenter Reservoir. His efforts had lowered the reservoir by May, but the inflows continued, and the water level again rose. Complicating the situation was that Hydro had shut down some of the turbines at Bridge River as well as the Seton powerhouse to do maintenance work. Those turbines got back into operation by June 15.

According to court records, by mid-July the inflows started to get out of control. Hydro biologist Owen Fleming recommended a large but short spill that would end before salmon spawning season began. The spill in late July went for several days and staff began to salvage any fish they could. But then a second spill was required due to a rainstorm that hit the coast hard between August 7 and August 12. Because

Stewart was working at the site, decisions on the spills were transferred to him. Later that month, another severe rainstorm led to another spill. The narrow river channel banks were scoured, driving dirty water downstream into the fish habitat and harming the spawning fish. Hydro scrambled to do damage control, stunning fish that were trapped in pools of water, air lifting them out, and relocating them.

Fisheries biologist Hugh Smith remembers the effort: "We had twenty-seven biologists running around trying to collect the fish that were stranded as the river dropped. Nobody in the world has done anything like that. We spent $330,000 on it. It was mostly for helicopter time, running up and down the river, trying to collect fish as they were being stranded and the DFO were behind us counting the dead fish. That's the sort of stress our staff was under."

Sometime later, DFO enforcement agents paid a visit to both the Bridge River and Kamloops offices with search warrants that gave them authority to look at Hydro files and computers. They even looked through the garbage cans. "It was indeed a big deal," says Don Swoboda. "Hydro had nothing to hide, and they were free to check our files for evidence as required."

DFO officers carried side arms on both raids and Stewart says he assured the officers that the guns weren't necessary — all Hydro staff were keen to cooperate, and the officers could conduct their search. The officers obliged by returning their weapons to their locked vehicles.

BC Hydro faced three charges at Terzaghi Dam under the Fisheries Act, for spills that occurred between July 25 and September 10, 1991. Those charges included the harmful disruption of fish habitat, the deposit of a deleterious substance (sediment sourced from the river bank) into fish habitat, and the killing of fish. Hydro faced two more similar charges for spills at Seton Dam that September. The Crown corporation was facing the maximum penalty of $1 million for each offence that had occurred on the Bridge and Seton Rivers. Some of the arguments that Hydro used as a defence included the fact that the minister of fisheries and oceans had authorized the spills that led to the charges, Hydro had acted with due diligence, the spills were necessary, and the reason for the spills was an act of nature. Stewart was not charged. "That was a big relief," he says. "That hung over our family for about five years, because until the actual charges were laid and we went to trial, we didn't know whether or not we would be individually charged. The thing is, you don't know what the potential consequences are. Throughout I held onto my belief that I was doing everything reasonable and possible to get the best outcome. I knew I had done nothing wrong. That's what I held onto. I hadn't misled anybody."

At hearings held between 1996 and 1997, Stewart felt a sense of relief because he got to tell his story. He believes the other Hydro employees felt the same way. "I can't imagine a better group of people. They worked tirelessly throughout this process."

Hydro was exonerated and the charges were dismissed. "I find that Hydro exercised due diligence with respect to the operation of the Seton and Terzaghi Dams and that accordingly it must be found not guilty on all counts in the indictment," said Judge G.W. Lamperson in his verdict.[5]

But the experience of this spill and the charges brought corporate changes with a focus on conservation initiatives. Hydro launched a gravel replacement program to help the fish spawn, and completed a study to find ways to release water from Terzaghi Dam without interfering with the salmon habitat. The company later embarked on a study to help steelhead stocks on the Fraser, Bridge and Seton Rivers. By the mid-1990s, the company had formed a steering committee that recognized a company-wide approach to dealing with matters of fish stocks.

The Strategic Fisheries Project was launched in 1994. The project's mandate was to study how hydroelectricity projects impacted fish resources throughout the province, with the aim being to protect fish species and habitat while producing electricity that would meet consumer needs. The production of electricity requires the storing of water and the releasing of it through turbines and over spillways. The flow of water varies throughout the seasons, and even the time of day, according to demand. That means the flow and quantity of water released fluctuates, which has a direct impact on streams and rivers, which affects fish spawning channels. The project identified measures that protected those facilities and established hatcheries. It also identified sites that needed the most improvement where fishery protection was concerned. An example of improvement might be increasing water flow at one project site, to encourage the salmon to return to spawning beds by the fall.

Hugh Smith, now retired after thirty-two years with BC Hydro, had put together the Strategic Fisheries Project team. "We looked at overall issues and potential solutions, and we recognized fairly early on that integrated watershed management was necessary," says Smith. There had been "major conflicts" over water use and salmon, and Smith needed to find a balance that worked for everyone, working with the provincial government, BC Hydro, the DFO and First Nations groups. "Once we defined the issues, we brought everybody together around a table, and went through a process of identifying each issue and quantifying how the operation of the system worked, and the implications to that objective."

In order to work, everyone had to agree on trade-offs they were willing to make. For example, BC Hydro monitored surfing quality at Port Renfrew on Vancouver Island as part of the 2011 Jordan River water use plan (WUP), due to community concerns about the popular watersport. Trying to arrive at consensus was a complex process. "The water use plan was about integrating all interests," says Smith. "We had as many as twenty different people at some tables, so everybody had to understand everybody else's interests to make the trade-offs that had to be made—that's why the process was so powerful. You'd think, 'I'm not here to maximize power. I'm here to maximize fish.' It was about optimizing the resources in the basin. In some cases, you had to trade off power for fish, or maybe fish for heritage issues for the First Nations. All those trade-offs were made. I spent ten years of my life doing water use planning. It was very demanding."

The team ran through a series of alternate scenarios to determine performance outcomes. It took the better part of ten years to achieve all the water use plans for each stakeholder on each watershed. They had a budget of $50 million.

ABOVE Announcement of the first 50-cubic-feet-per-second permanent water release past Terzaghi Dam, summer 1998. Tsal'alh chief Qwalqwalten (Garry John) with BC Hydro representative Terry Molstad to the right. In the background are Shawn Casper and Richard Casper, who were young Tsal'alhmec at the time. Courtesy of Don Swoboda

Retreating Glacier

The Bridge River project is remarkable not just for its technical complexity and scale, but because the source of the water flowing into it is a massive glacier that sits within BC's Coast Mountain range. That glacier water is the reason that Carpenter Lake Reservoir is a bright, milky green colour. It's also the reason that Seton Lake is a similar colour, unlike Anderson Lake next to it, which remains naturally clear.

The hydroelectric site was chosen largely because of the seasonal differences between the river valley and earlier projects at Buntzen, Stave Lake and Alouette. The glacier-fed Bridge River project is the perfect complement to the coastal lake projects, where water is largely derived from rainfall. Bridge River runoff, measured in cubic feet per second, soars in the summer months of July and August and drops off in the fall and winter months, as temperatures drop and runoff waters freeze. That means that Bridge River could carry the bulk of the load during the summer and early fall, with the full reservoirs at Stave, Buntzen and Alouette Lakes supplying water to the power plants the remainder of the year.

But like most of the world's glaciers, Bridge Glacier is shrinking, and it's retreating at a startling rate — an estimated two miles (3.5 km) in the last four decades, according to experts. Scientist Garry Clarke's estimation that 70 percent of glaciers in BC and Alberta will be gone by the year 2100 is the generally held belief for those who study glaciers, and who are witnessing first-hand that the snow packs that turn to ice in the winter are decreasing, while the runoffs in spring are increasing. The area is receiving more rainfall than snow, and that's an issue.

BC Hydro hydrometeorologic field programs scientist Frank Weber is one of a large team that is monitoring the glacier to determine the balance of runoff in summer and winter months. As well, UBC students take measurements and place markers to determine whether they've gained or lost ice on the glacier, and how much. Weber says Hydro also monitors the glacier by plane, and they know it's decreasing. "When we do climate change impact studies we project out several decades what the flows will be into the reservoirs," says Weber. "You need to understand pretty well how the glaciers behave, and what they have done.

"We try to get a handle on water resources in these watersheds. Right now, we are withdrawing money from the bank, so to speak. We are melting ice slowly off, and that might be good for hydroelectricity in the short term, but it changes things when hydrology changes later on. There's less summer runoff, which may not be an issue for hydroelectricity because it's only part of the total. But if you didn't have that ice melt, the rivers would become very dry, and the flows would lower in late summer periods. And that does have impact on the ecology, keeping rivers in BC cold enough for salmon and also other species in rivers."

It's a situation that is of concern to Gerald Michel, fisheries and land use coordinator for the Xwisten. If the spring runoff isn't cold enough, and if it gets above 68°F (20°C), young salmon can catch infectious diseases and die. Adult salmon that return from the ocean to the Fraser River to spawn might not live long enough to lay their eggs. And as the glaciers of BC disappear or considerably shrink, the majestic snow-capped mountains will visually transform. BC will be a very different looking province.

The Water Use Planning project won many awards and was lauded as progressive and novel by organizations around the world. Smith travelled to places like Beijing and Siberia to give presentations on their work.

BC Hydro president Chris O'Riley says the DFO ordeal shaped the current culture in two crucial ways: it led to the series of settlement agreements in 2011 with the St'át'imc, and it led to the progressive Water Use Planning Program being implemented throughout BC, which was a shift in thinking away from the idea of water use for purely economic purposes, as it had been seen for decades, to one that looked at the social and environmental implications as well. The program was designed in partnership with the First Nations, the DFO and provincial regulators.

"We would figure out within bounds what the best way was to use water, and it resulted in changes in flows at certain places, including at Bridge," says O'Riley. "As well, there were compensation programs, and monitoring programs, at Bridge. We did those all around the province. They started in the nineties, and they are just coming up for renewal today. That all started as a result of those flow issues of the early nineties."

8

An Agreement for St'át'imc Reconciliation

BC Hydro and the province entered negotiations with the St'át'imc Chiefs Council, an association of chiefs from all of the St'át'imc communities, in 1993 that would ultimately lead to a series of agreements that would define the relationship between the parties for generations to come. The St'át'imc Chiefs Council represented eleven Indigenous communities and about 6,000 members over a large geographical area, including the Xa'xtsa First Nation, whose Port Douglas and Tipella Reserves are located at the northern edge of Harrison Lake; the Skatin First Nation, whose territory is located along the Lillooet River; and the Samahquam First Nation, whose Baptiste Smith Reserve is located near the southern end of Lillooet Lake.

In the early 1990s, BC Hydro was facing a significant rehabilitation program for the aging Bridge River system facilities and was looking for business certainty. The first of a long list of replacements would start in 2003 with the replacement of the Bridge 1 transformers. The St'át'imc were committed to address a number of past, present and potentially future grievances related to the impacts of the facilities on their traditional territories and, in addition to the preservation of their culture and historical food sources such as the salmon, they wanted to develop their own economy.

The "agreement" is actually a package of eighteen separate agreements negotiated over a period of seventeen years. These agreements include a relations agreement to govern the future relationship between St'át'imc and BC Hydro. The reconciliation package of agreements with the St'át'imc was completed in May 2011. There are three key main agreements — the Settlement Agreement, the Certainty Provisions Agreement and the Relations Agreement — and eleven separate community agreements. These agreements provide for:

- Long term environmental mitigation plans to help restore land, water, fish, wildlife and vegetation;

- A heritage and culture plan to preserve, protect and promote St'át'imc culture;

- A relations agreement to assist in developing a long-term sustainable relationship between the St'át'imc and BC Hydro;

- An education and training component to build capacity within the communities; and

- A financial package, worth more than $200 million in total, providing money for a trust fund to be paid out over ninety-nine years.

VOICES FROM BRIDGE RIVER

It was an ambitious undertaking. BC Hydro president Chris O'Riley says his most important role at Bridge River is improving BC Hydro's relationship with the First Nations communities that live there, and he acknowledges that those relationships are still a work in progress. BC Hydro, he says, takes responsibility for the actions of its predecessor company, BC Electric, and says it's now their job to right the wrongs of the past, as difficult as that might be. Across the province, by 2011, BC Hydro had entered into comprehensive settlement agreements with three First Nations groups that aimed to do that very thing.

Three years after these agreements were signed, on March 3, 2014, the province, separately, entered into a revenue sharing agreement with the Xwisten (Bridge River) Band in respect to sharing provincial revenues from land revenues and water rentals from clean energy projects as defined under the Clean Energy Act.

One of the early results of the BC Hydro and St'át'imc negotiations was the approval of BC Hydro's application to the BC Utilities Commission to interconnect the southern St'át'imc communities to the transmission electrical system in the Lillooet River/Harrison Lake corridor. BC Hydro and the St'át'imc are also collaborating on water use planning. The two parties are working together to protect water quality, riparian habitat and fisheries.

FACING Location of the permanent water release past the Terzaghi Dam in the summer of 1998. Note the low-level outlet immediately below the spillway. Rod Louie, former lead negotiator of BC Hydro/St'át'imc negotiations and member of the Tsal'alh First Nation (*far right*) is briefing the book team (*right to left*): writer Kerry Gold, Don Swoboda of the Power Pioneers, Kerry's husband Mike Elsinga, and Bryan Bodell of the Power Pioneers. Courtesy of Jim Gemmill
BELOW Opened in 2016, the Lil'tem' Mountain Hotel features forty-two rooms equipped with kitchenettes. The property is part of a St'át'imc initiative to build a tourist industry in the area. Courtesy of Jim Gemmill

All of the parties have started out with high expectations, but the complexity of the agreements and turnover of staff on both sides has made the initial implementation phase of the agreements challenging.

Chris O'Riley has discovered that attempts to create agreements aimed at fixing the past have proven far more challenging to implement than agreements designed with only future collaborations in mind. Much smaller agreements made with other First Nations communities have proven far more successful. "Our goal in these relationships is that they are hugely beneficial, and they [the St'át'imc] feel fulfilled from the relationship."

Before he retired, Bryan Bodell was Indigenous relations coordinator at BC Hydro, and he focused on forging relationships with First Nations communities throughout the province. He says that through intense effort, and trial and error, Hydro has set a high bar for itself for reconciliation with First Nations groups. "BC Hydro endeavours to be a leader in developing mutually beneficial relationships with Indigenous people, communities and businesses," he says.

The St'át'imc have been very proactive in developing their own economy. Eco Resources was set up for business opportunities for the many service, administrative and supply companies run by the St'át'imc. The grand Lil'tem' Mountain

Hotel in Seton Portage was built by the Tsal'alh (Seton Lake), who are also known as People of the Lake. They are one of the communities within the St'át'imc Nation, and BC Hydro's Bridge River facility is their direct neighbour. Hydro is committed to using the hotel for its workers during the prolonged upgrade to the Bridge River systems, over the next decade. The Tsal'alh are also investigating the future use of the Lil'tem' Mountain Hotel as part of a destination recreation business for the area to provide jobs and economic benefits.

St'át'imc members have taken some jobs on the crews doing the upgrades, and have been awarded contracts associated with the projects and operational support. The community is working with the Crown corporation on safety issues, particularly road safety on the Highline Road, between D'Arcy and Seton Portage, and over Mission Mountain, which are still hazardous journeys in poor weather. Hydro is also offering scholarships for St'át'imc youth and to secondary students in Lillooet who are interested in training in science, math and the trades.

When former Tsal'alh chief Ida Mary Peter suggested the giant penstock supports could use a little beautification with Indigenous murals, Hydro's project manager Jim Shepherd helped facilitate the hiring of a local artist to get the artwork done.

Michelle Edwards is chief of the Sekw'el'was (Cayoose Creek) Band. She was instrumental in the negotiation and ratification of the St'át'imc–Hydro Settlement Agreement and is active in many aspects of the implementation of the various agreements.

The Sekw'el'was Band is making major inroads into true stewardship of their territory. Chief Edwards announced early in 2019 that they'd entered into a partnership with a Vancouver-based engineering firm to build infrastructure such as water, sewer, roads and facilities, both on and off reserve. The band has a business arm, the Cayoose Creek Development Corporation (CCDC), which owns a subsidiary company called Antares, which develops infrastructure projects. In 2016, they purchased the Walden North hydroelectric project, a 16-megawatt run-of-river plant that diverts water from Cayoosh Creek. They sell the electricity to BC Hydro.

Rod Louie was the director of operations for the St'át'imc Chiefs Council from 2011 to 2014.

FACING BC Hydro local management and the Tsal'alh collaborated to display artwork on the Bridge 2 penstock pedestals and the initiative is representative of the developing working relationship between them. Raymond Alexander is the artist. The artwork includes the traditional St'át'imc name of each animal beside the depictions. Courtesy of Rod Louie

171

LEFT The Sk'il' Mountain Community School was established in 2000 on the road between Shalalth and Seton Portage. The school has thirteen full-time staff who teach blended classrooms from kindergarten to grade twelve. Operated by the Tsal'alh government, the school integrates the language and culture of the Tsal'alh with the district curriculum. Courtesy of Rod Louie
BELOW Fran Shields teaching the next generation, Veronica Shields-Joseph, with Bryan Bodell in the background, processing deer meat at the Sk'il' Mountain Community School. Courtesy of Jim Gemmill

He also sees economic opportunities for Shalalth, such as tourism. Even without promotion, the remote beauty of the region is already a draw for world travellers. The BBC declared the Kaoham Shuttle train journey between Seton Portage and Lillooet "Canada's greatest hidden rail trip," for the views from its windows as it hugs the shore of Seton Lake. And wilderness-loving urbanites are travelling into remote regions in search of hiking, rock climbing, horse trail riding, mountain biking and kayaking. The community is looking to tap into those tourist markets, which are less intrusive to the environment than previous industries.

Notwithstanding all the progress made, there are current issues that are challenging to the relationship. Perry Redan, who served as the Sekw'el'was chief for twenty years, says that from the St'át'imc's perspective the big issue that the 2011 agreements did not address was the schedule for a future Lajoie Dam upgrade.

In order to manage the reservoir until the dam's seismic upgrade can be done, the water of Downton Reservoir had to be lowered in 2015 and that triggered a chain reaction. The fish habitat in the lower Bridge River depends on a specific predetermined flow of water that was established in the collaborative water use planning process with the St'át'imc, and when that flow is altered, the resulting high water flows and erosion can wreak havoc with the salmon spawning grounds. "We are trying to work out a faster process in getting Lajoie repaired," says Redan. BC Hydro and the St'át'imc have now set up a joint planning forum with St'át'imc representatives to better incorporate St'át'imc interests into these complex water management processes.

Jim Scouras, BC Hydro's Indigenous Relations Manager for southeastern BC, says reconciliation is not an easy fix. "We all continue to work at it, and it's going to take time and the commitment of all of the parties."

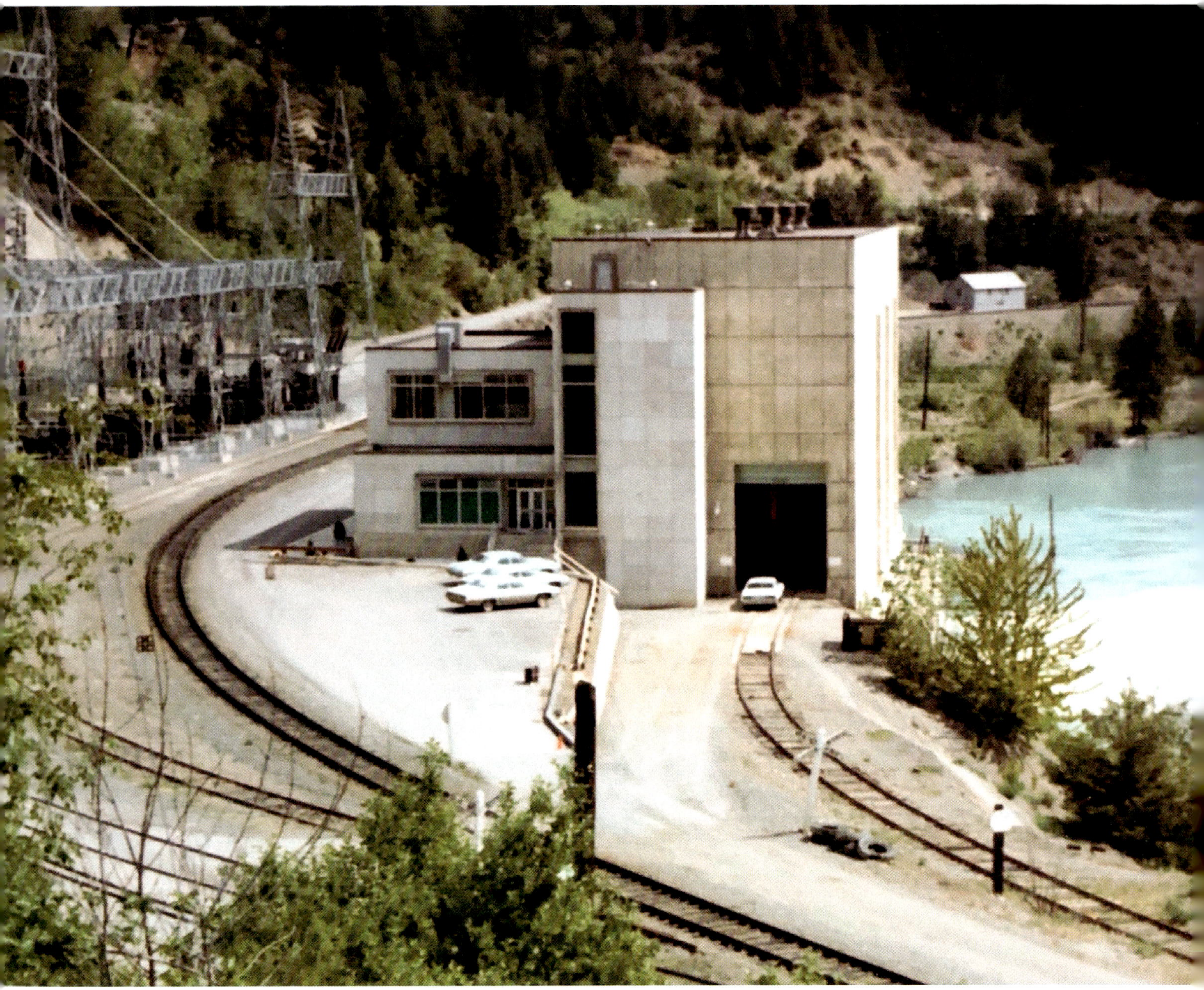

Epilogue: A Work in Progress

From its conception on that summer day in 1912 when Geoffrey Downton and Patrick Dick Booth, standing on Mission Ridge, noted the elevation difference between the Bridge River Valley and Seton Lake, to the present day, the Bridge River hydroelectric development is a story of epic proportions. Not only was it a magnificent engineering feat, it would usher in an era of publicly owned power in BC and the beginning of the postwar boom.

Development of the Bridge River system pushed technical boundaries in an era of slide rules and survey equipment, unaided by modern GPS and laser technology. It was also a triumph of political and financial will, surviving through two world wars and the Great Depression to emerge as a critical supply of electricity, providing half of the needs of the Lower Mainland on its completion in 1960. Few projects can claim to have succeeded through so many technical and political challenges over a 100-year period.

Bridge is now going through a renaissance of its own. Bridge 1 was completed in 1948 and its sister plant Bridge 2 was completed in 1960. Although the Bridge River system has moved from supplying half of the needs of the Lower Mainland to more like 5 percent of BC Hydro's total needs today, the combined output still equates to approximately half of a Site C, which is currently under construction on the Peace River. If Bridge River were no longer available to BC Hydro, there would be a deficit of about 2,300 gigawatt hours of energy which, if met with natural gas generation, would produce over 1.5 million metric tons of carbon dioxide per year.[1]

A major refurbishment is underway to ensure the reliable supply of electricity from these facilities well into the future. BC Hydro is spending almost $700 million on various projects, starting with new Pelton impulse turbines for Bridge 2 Units 5 and 6 (completed in 2001) and Bridge 1 impulse turbines 1 through 4 (completed in 2003). Replacement transformer installations for Bridge 1 were completed in 2017. Replacement of the Bridge 2 Units 5 and 6 generators were completed in 2019.

These upgrades will be followed by a number of projects over the next twenty years to ensure the continued reliability of this important energy source. The table on the next page illustrates the scope of these projects based on the best available estimates in mid-2021.

FACING Bridge 1, the mothership of the Bridge River system, circa 1975. Courtesy of Bob Nelless

Bridge River System Capital Upgrades Plan (2021 Estimates)

START	ESTIMATED COMPLETION	FACILITY	EQUIPMENT
	2001	BR 2	Units 5 & 6 turbine replacements
	2003	BR 1	Units 1 to 4 turbine replacements
2014	2017	BR 1	Station transformer replacements: from six single-phase transformers to two three-phase transformers
2012	2019	BR 2	Units 5 and 6 generator replacements
2016	2018		Concurrent penstock interior recoating
2015	2021	BR 2	Units 7 and 8 generator replacements
2016	2018		Concurrent internal penstock recoating
2016	2023	BRT	Transformer replacements
2018	2025	BRT	Thermal upgrade of transmission line from Bridge River Terminal to Kelly Lake Terminal
2018	2025	Seton	Refurbishment of generator and plant
2018	2026	Lajoie	Dam seismic upgrades
2023	2030+	Terzaghi Dam	Low-level discharge reliability
2015	2028	BR 1	Units 1 to 4 generator replacements Concurrent internal penstock recoating
2026	2030	Lajoie	Generator replacement: planning stage
2018	2029–30	Lajoie	Dam seismic upgrades: conceptual design stage
2023	2029	Seton	Canal flow control structure upgrade
2030+	TBD	Seton	Dam improvements

Refurbished Bridge 1 units. Courtesy of Jim Gemmill

In the meantime, the Lajoie Dam has been in the plan for seismic upgrades as part of the overall Bridge River facilities program. However, in the fall of 2014 BC Hydro, having completed a review of all of its dams around the province, lowered the water level in Downton Reservoir as a precaution, to manage the seismic risk. Once the Bridge 1 generator replacements are completed in 2028, seismic upgrades to the Lajoie Dam will commence with a current target completion of 2029–30. This will mark the substantial completion of the Bridge River rehabilitation project with a lower level of activity on ancillary projects into the future.

The current rehabilitation work, involving unit replacements and the planned upgrade of the Lajoie Dam, is a complex endeavour, particularly when it comes to the management of water flows. The lowering of water levels in reservoirs and removal of generating units from service results in significant departures from normal management of high inflows and makes the system particularly vulnerable to weather events. There are few alternatives to redirect water, so extreme rain or spring freshets may result in high water flows down the Bridge River Valley, with potentially destructive impacts on salmon spawning grounds downstream. Events have already demonstrated the level of planning and diligence required to limit these impacts.

Jim Shepherd is a mechanical engineer and project manager who oversees seven project managers who work on projects throughout the province, including Bridge River. He says the seismic upgrade and structural work on Lajoie Dam will cost more than the cost of upgrading the two Bridge 1 and 2 power plants combined. He oversees a team of engineers and construction workers and he's been working on upgrades at Bridge River since he started in 2007.

"Within the Bridge River facilities we have [a] sixty-to-seventy-year-old system of equipment running twenty-four hours a day, seven days a week. The generators run about two years before they are taken out of service for regular maintenance. Those machines run hard all the time, and so eventually they wear to the point that replacement is the only option. To me, my biggest success as a project manager within this region would be to ensure that we complete the work safely — no injuries — and ensure that the people within the region are adequately represented in the staffing and the crews that are doing the work. That is what we are trying to achieve."

The Bridge River system is now entering a new phase in its life as the facilities rehabilitation proceeds to completion. The initiatives and efforts by all parties to restore salmon runs and provide local economic development will hopefully be a lasting legacy for the people of the valley, while the Bridge River system continues to provide much needed clean electricity to the province for generations to come.

Acknowledgements

We acknowledge that this book takes place in the unceded traditional territory of the St'át'imc, representing eleven Indigenous communities from Lillooet to Harrison Lake. Our thanks to Rod Louie, director of operations for the St'át'imc Chiefs Council from 2011 to 2014 and currently chief executive officer at Tsal'alh Development Corporation, for his assistance.

The BC Hydro Power Pioneers represent 2,000 BC Hydro retirees who are committed to preserving the history of electricity in British Columbia, a resource that has brought prosperity to the province and a standard of living that we may take for granted today. The Power Pioneers are also committed to giving back to their communities. The proceeds from the sale of their historical books go to BC Children's Hospital through their Miracle Millions Campaign.

Special thanks go to the Power Pioneers team that has contributed to the creation of these books: Bryan Bodell, Lorilee Koltai, Phil Horton, Don Swoboda and project manager Jim Gemmill, who shepherded the team through to completion.

Pat Crawford made a major contribution throughout the book, sorting through hundreds of images from BC Hydro's archives. The book also benefited from images and research provided by Susan Medville (Mountain Heritage) who was doing research on behalf of the St'át'imc. Many others made contributions from their personal photo collections to bring life to the oral history of this book.

Thanks to all of those who shared their technical knowledge of the Bridge River development, particularly Hugh Smith of BC Hydro's environmental department who provided critical insights into the impacts on the salmon through the life of the projects. Similarly, Odin Scholz of Splitrock Environmental, a Cayoose Band subsidiary, has been a big help in providing pictures and information for the Seton spawning channel as the company's senior biologist.

Also, thanks to our writer, Kerry Gold, who produced a draft manuscript that reflected the incredible complexity of the Bridge River area while incorporating the voices of those who have lived in the area from time immemorial to the present.

Thanks as well to everyone at Figure 1 Publishing. Chris Labonté and Lara Smith supervised the project for Figure 1, with Pam Robertson, copy editor, and Renate Preuss, proofreader, making significant contributions to the quality of the final manuscript and the finished book.

Finally, thanks go out to all those who gave so generously of their recollections and insights. Those who shared their stories and photos give a voice to so many people the Bridge River has touched over the ages.

Notes

Introduction
1. *The BC Electric Family Post*, vol. 44, no. 13, July 15, 1960.
2. Ibid.

1: Potential Power
1. Evenden, Matthew D., *Fish versus Power: An Environmental History of the Fraser River* (Cambridge, UK: Cambridge University Press, 2004), p. 79.
2. Akrigg, G.P.V. and Helen B. Akrigg, *British Columbia Place Names* (Vancouver: UBC Press, 1997).
3. *British Columbia Gazette*, January 2, 1913.
4. Ibid.
5. Ibid.
6. Vancouver City Council minutes, November 29, 1916.
7. *British Columbia Historical News* (Spring 1994), p. 10.
8. Maiden, Cecil, *Lighted Journey: The Story of BC Electric* (Vancouver: BC Electric, 1948), p. 44.
9. Maiden, p. 47.
10. Evenden, p. 64.
11. Maiden, p. 89.
12. Maiden, p. 108.
13. Maiden, p. 105.
14. BC Electric Railway Company, *The Bridge River Power Development*, booklet, circa 1930.

2: Construction Begins
1. BCER, *The Bridge River Power Development*, booklet, circa 1930, p. 13.
2. Maiden, Cecil, *Lighted Journey: The Story of BC Electric* (Vancouver: BC Electric, 1948), p. 113.
3. Green, Lewis, *The Great Years: Gold Mining in the Bridge River Valley* (Vancouver: Tricouni Press, 2000), p. 84.
4. Cotton, Barry, "The Buntzen Lake Project, 1901 to 1906," *British Columbia Historical News* (Fall 2003).
5. Green, *The Great Years*, p. 80.
6. Wikipedia, "Herbert Samuel Holt," accessed at https://en.wikipedia.org/wiki/Herbert_Samuel_Holt.
7. Galloway, J.D., *Report on the Mainland Power Situation of the B.C. Electrical Co. Ltd., and the Proposed Bridge River Power Development Ltd.*, February 17, 1925.
8. BCER, *Intercom*, company newsletter, February 13, 1974.
9. Maiden, p. 117.
10. Maiden, p. 123.
11. Maiden, p. 125.
12. de Hullu, Emma, *Bridge River Gold* (Bralorne, BC: Bralorne Pioneer Community Club, 1967).
13. *Electrical West* magazine, November 1934.
14. Maiden, p. 133.

3: Valley of Plenty
1. Sahlins, Marshall, *Stone Age Economics* (Abingdon, UK: Routledge, 2017, originally published 1972).
2. "Assessing BC Hydro's Impacts to St'át'imc Society and Culture," Part I of a joint report prepared for St'át'imc Nation Hydro Committee. Lillooet, BC, June 2005.
3. Edwards, Irene, *Short Portage to Lillooet & Other Trails and Tales* (Stanley Printing Co., 1978), p. 77.
4. Edwards, p. 80.
5. Drake-Terry, Joanne, *The Same As Yesterday: The Lillooet Chronicle the Theft of their Lands and Resources* (Lillooet Tribal Council, 1989), p. 36.
6. James Douglas to Henry Labouchère, "Despatch to London," July 15, 1857. Accessed at https://bcgenesis.uvic.ca/V57022.html.
7. St'át'imc Government Services website, "Territory History," accessed at https://statimc.ca/about-us/history/.
8. Drake-Terry, p. xvi.
9. Edwards, p. 169.

4: Bridge River Internment Camp

1. Gomer Sunahara, Ann, *The Politics of Racism: The Uprooting of Japanese Canadians During the Second World War* (Toronto: Lorimer, 1981), p. 45.
2. Gomer Sunahara, *The Politics of Racism*, chapter 3, accessed at http://japanesecanadianhistory.ca/chapter-3-expulsion.
3. Saimoto, Ritsu, "A Tribute," from the booklet *Sentimental Journey, 50th Anniversary, October 9, 1992*, produced by the Bridge River/Devine/Lillooet/Minto Reunion Committee.
4. Miyazaki, Masajiro, *My Sixty Years in Canada* (Lillooet: self-published, 1973).
5. Miyazaki, *My Sixty Years in Canada*.
6. Enjo, Den, "Boyhood Recollections of East Lillooet," from the booklet *Sentimental Journey, 50th Anniversary, October 9, 1992*, produced by the Bridge River/Devine/Lillooet/Minto Reunion Committee.
7. Miyazaki, *My Sixty Years in Canada*.
8. Miyazaki, *My Sixty Years in Canada*.
9. Saimoto, "A Tribute."
10. See Pat Carney's column in the *Province*, Thursday, May 17, 1962.

5: The Construction Era

1. Akrigg, G.P.V. and Helen B. Akrigg, *British Columbia Place Names* (Vancouver: UBC Press, 1997).
2. Evenden, Matthew D., *Fish versus Power: An Environmental History of the Fraser River* (Cambridge, UK: Cambridge University Press, 2004), p. 130.
3. BCER, *The Bridge River Power Development*, booklet, circa 1930.
4. Evenden, p. 122.
5. Evenden, p. 129.
6. Maiden, Cecil, *Lighted Journey: The Story of BC Electric* (Vancouver: BC Electric, 1948), p. 160.
7. Maiden, p. 160.
8. Maiden, p. 167.
9. Maiden, p. 169.
10. Goodman, Richard E., *Karl Terzaghi: The Engineer as Artist* (Reston, VA: ASCE Press, 1998), pp. 266–67.
11. Goodman, p. 272.
12. Goodman, p. 273.
13. In Taylor, H., "Performance of Terzaghi Dam 1960 to 1969," a paper for the Seventh International Conference on Soil Mechanics and Geotechnical Engineering, Mexico, 1969.
14. Evenden, *Fish versus Power*.
15. Grauer, Dal, *BC Electric Family Post*, November 1, 1948.
16. Parry, Malcolm, "Town Talk," *Vancouver Sun*, December 30, 2000.
17. *BC Power Corporation Annual Report*, 1957, p. 4.
18. Young, Harry, "Takeover Supported," *Victoria Daily Colonist*, October 22, 1961.

7: The Impacts

1. de Hullu, Emma, *Bridge River Gold* (Bralorne, BC: Bralorne Pioneer Community Club, 1967), p. 84.
2. Cleven, Mike, "Upper Bridge River Valley Before Flooding: A Personal Memento," posted on bivouac.com.
3. Andrew, F.J. and G.H. Geen, *Sockeye and Pink Salmon Investigations at the Seton Creek Hydroelectric Installation* (New Westminster, BC: International Pacific Salmon Fisheries Commission, 1958).
4. Andrew and Geen, p. 34.
5. BC Supreme Court judgement, Her Majesty the Queen v. British Columbia Hydro and Power Authority [2007], accessed at www.bccourts.ca/jdb-txt/sc/97/10/s97-1090.txt.

Epilogue

1. Per the US EPA Greenhouse Gas Equivalency Calculator for combined cycle gas turbine.

Index

Photos and drawings indicated by page numbers in italics

A

Adolph, Isaac, 48
Adrian, Marcel, *46*
aircraft, Grumman Goose, 24, *26*
Alaska Highway News, 69
Alcan (formerly Aluminum Company of Canada), 72, 76
Alexander, Carl, *50*, 51
Alexander, Raymond, *171*
Alouette Lake power project, 15, 16, 22, 29, 31, 164. *See also* Ruskin power project; Stave Lake (Stave Falls) power project
aluminum production, 72, 76
ambulance, for Lillooet, *64*, 64-65
American Nitrogen, 13
Anderson, Alexander, 40
Anderson Lake, x, 99, 118, 147, 154, 164
Andrew, F.J., 154
Annacis Island, 115
Anscomb, Herbert, 102
Antares, 170
Ashcroft (BC), 60, 65, 113-14, 131
Atkins, Jackie, *138*, 142
Atkins, Russ, *136*

B

Bank of Montreal, 14
Barker, Billy, 40
Barkerville (BC), 40, 41
Barnard, Francis, 41
Barnard, Frank Stillman, 10, 11, 12, 27, 31, 35, 41
Bata Shoe Company, 159
BC Electric (BCE; formerly BC Electric Railway (BCER)): about, xiv, xv; acquisition of Bridge River Power Company, 7, 14, 16, 125; attempts to attract federal funding, 72-73; Bridge River relaunch during gold rush, 32-33; Bridge River relaunch post-WWII, 77-78, 79, 128; "Business Is Moving to BC" campaign, 75-76; competition with Western Canada Power Company, 14-15; Depression and, 31-32; donation for Lillooet ambulance, 65; expansion into Thompson River region, 113-14; expropriation concerns, 72, 75, 105; expropriation of, 122, 123, 132; expropriation of Indigenous land by, 39; fish stocks and, 153-54, 157; formation of, 10, 12, 41; Grauer and, 34, 35, 71, 76, 128; growth and expansion, 12-13, 16, 77, 108, 112-13, 115-16; *Homemakers* radio show, 31-32; hostile takeover by Montreal syndicate, 26-27; initial attempt to purchase Bridge River project, 6-7; jubilee celebrations, 76-77; leadership changes, 27, 71, 76; name change, xiv; organizational splits, 71; promotion of Bridge River project, 18-19, 103-5; Second World War and, 35, 37; shareholders, 116; shift away from Bridge River, 27-29; thermal power projects, 29, 120, 121, 123, 154; Vancouver and, 13, 73. *See also* Alouette Lake power project; BC Hydro; BC Power Corporation; Bridge River power project; Buntzen Lake power project; Grauer, Albert Edward "Dal"; Ruskin power project; Stave Lake (Stave Falls) power project
BC Electric Family Post (magazine), 103-4
BC Electric Power Act (1945), 78
BC Energy Board, 121
BC Energy Plan, 121
BC Express Company, 41
BC Game Commission, 153
BC Hydro: agreements with St'át'imc Nation, 165, 167-70, 173; Carpenter Lake cleanup, 151-53; emergency spills and, 158-62; fish stocks and, 48, 162-63; formation of, xiv, 122, 123; Indigenous peoples and, 168, 169; Ma Murray against, 69; snow camp and, 59; Water Use Planning project, 162-63, 165. *See also* BC Electric; Bridge River power project
BC Motor Transportation Limited, 71, 77
BC Power Commission: amalgamation with BC Electric, xv, 122, 123, 132; BC Electric Railway relations, 102-3, 113; development projects and rural electrification, 78, 105; formation and purpose, 78, 122; Powell River district and, 115; power supply to Bridge River region, 61
BC Power Corporation: on Alcan's Kitimat project, 76; BC Electric Railway reorganization and, 71; BC Power Commission and, 78; development projects, 116, 121; expropriation of BC Electric and, 123; formation of, 27; Hat Creek coal deposits and, 121; Peace River Power Development Company and, 120; power exports to US, 112. *See also* BC Electric
BC Rail, 60, 145. *See also* Pacific Great Eastern (PGE) Railway

BC Security Commission, 53, 54, 56, 60, 62, 63, 127
BC Tel, 59
Bennett, W.A.C. (Bennett government): Columbia and Peace Rivers power projects ("Two Rivers Policy"), 121, 122, 154-55; expropriation of BC Electric, 122, 123; Ma Murray against, 68, 69; photograph, *75*; Post-War Rehabilitation Council and, 74
Blacksmith Hill, 128
Blee, C.E., *17*
bobsleds, 138, *139*, 141
Bodell, Bryan, *36*, *168*, 169, *172*
Bodley, John, 39
Bonnycastle, W.R., 4, 5, 6, 14, *17*, 29
Booth, Patrick Dick, 3, 4, *5*, 6, 175
Booth & Downton, 5
Braden, N.S., 7
Bralorne and Bralorne mines: gold rush and, 32, 42; mine ownership, 32, 53; power service to, xi, 33, 71, 116, 119, 125-26, 131; road to, 24, 59, 149
Bridge Glacier, 164-65
Bridge River, ix
Bridge River (townsite): about, xi, xv, 125; 1960-1980 community life, 132-34, 135-38, 141-42; bobsleds, 138, *139*, 141; closure after staff reductions, *146*, 146-47; dances, 137, 142; establishment, 21; first aid and medical services, 56, 57-58, 137; Japanese Canadian internment, 53, 54-55, 56-57, 60-61, 66, 127; miniature castle, 58, *58*, 147; schooling, 128, *129*, 142-45; after Second World War, 105, 128-30; before Second World War, 33, 125-26, *126*; during Second World War, 37; snow camp, 59; television, 136, *140*; tennis club, *129*, 134; travel to and from, 21, 24, 129-30, *130*, 131, 142, 144. *See also* Shalalth
Bridge River Barbershop Choir, *136*
Bridge River-Lillooet News, 68, 69
Bridge River Power Company, 5-7, 13, 16, 29, 125. *See also* Bridge River power project
The Bridge River Power Development (BCER booklet), 19
Bridge River power project: about, x-xii, *xii*, xiii-xiv, xv, 71, 120-21, 175, 178; acquisition by BC Electric Railway (BCER), 7, 14, 16, 125; attempts to attract federal funding, 72-73; Carpenter's presentation on, 29-30; completion and opening ceremonies, 100-103, *103*, 115-16, 120; construction challenges, 16-18; early development pre-WWI, 5-6; employment at, xii; expansion of, 106, 108; feasibility studies, 7, 16; Grauer and, 34, 103-5; inflow data, 29-30; Langley (formerly Burnaby Mountain) control centre, xi, 142, 146, 159; Montreal syndicate and, 6-7, 16; original vision and development concepts, *viii*, 3, 4, *18*, *19*, 49; penstocks, *92*, *93*, *93*, *109*, *170*, *171*; power generation, xi, 31, 112, 175; powerhouses, *94-95*, 94-96, *96*, 110-11, *111*, 120, *174*; promotion efforts, 18-19, 103-5; rehabilitation program, 167, 175-78, *177*; relaunch during gold rush, 32-33; relaunch post-WWII, 77-78, 79, 128; sidelined in favour of projects closer to Vancouver, 27-29; staffing, 135, 146; temporary powerhouse, xi, 33, *35*, 60, 125-26; tunnel construction, 21-23, 25, 26, 29, 31, 90, *91*; unrealized schemes, 13. *See also* environment; Lajoie Dam and powerhouse; Seton power project; St'át'imc Nation; Terzaghi Dam; transmission lines
Bridge River Valley, ix-x, 24, 32. *See also* Bralorne and Bralorne mines; Bridge River (townsite); Minto City; Pioneer mine
Brighton Beach (New Brighton Park, Vancouver), 29
British Columbia: centennial celebrations, *138*; engineers and surveyors, xiv-xv, 4-5; establishment, 42; expropriation of BC Electric, 72, 78, 105, 122, 123, 132; gold, ix, 9, 32, 40-42, 43, 125, 149; hydroelectric potential, 4; industrial development after WWII, 76; Post-War Rehabilitation Council, 72, 74-75, 78, 105; push for publicly owned power, 73-75; "Two Rivers Policy," 122, 154-55. *See also* BC Hydro; BC Power Commission; Japanese Canadian internment
British Columbia Gazette, 5, 6
British Empire Trust, 7
Brown, Harry, 101
Brunner, Doug, *88*
Budd Car (railway), 24, *25*, 128-29, 131, 134, 135, 142, 144-45
Bull, John, *45*
Bull, Tommy, 51
Buntzen, Johannes, 12-13
Buntzen Lake, 4
Buntzen Lake power project: Bridge River project and, 22, 30, 71, 164; development and rehabilitation, 12, 13, 23, 113; employment at, 58, 60, 126; nitric acid manufacturing, 13; power generation, 31, 94

Burnaby Mountain control centre, xi, 142, 159
Burrard Thermal plant, 120, 123, 134, 135
bus transit system, 71, 77, 116. *See also* interurban transit system; streetcars

C

Cahan, Charles H., 14
Canadian Imperial Bank of Commerce, 21, 125
Canadian National Railway, 60. *See also* BC Rail; Pacific Great Eastern (PGE) Railway
Canadian Northern Railway, 7, 10
Canadian Pacific Railway (CPR), 7, 10, 22, 101
carbide lamps, 25
Cariboo Gold Rush, 40–42. *See also* gold
Carpenter, E.E., xiii, 14, 15–16, *17*, 29–30, 95
Carpenter Lake Reservoir: cleanup efforts, 151–53; emergency spills, 158–62; environmental impacts and land flooded, xiii, 45, 149, 150–51; glacial water in, 164; Lajoie Dam and, 9, 88; photograph, *152*
Casagrande, Arthur, 81, 87
Casper, Richard, *163*
Casper, Shawn, *163*
castle, miniature, 58, *58*, 147
Cayoose Creek Development Corporation (CCDC), 170
Cheakamus hydroelectric project, 80, 112, 115
Christmas, 60, 129, *138*
Clarke, Garry, 164
Clean Energy Act, 168
Cleven, Andy, 151

Cleven, Mike, 79, 151
Clowhom hydroelectric project, 112, 115, 131
Colbourne, Neil, 137
colonialism: gold rushes and, 40–42, 43; Indian Act, 39, 42; land encroachment, 51, 158; residential schools, 43–44
Columbia and Kootenay Navigation Company, 10
Columbia River, 73–74, 160
Columbia River power project, 95, 121, 122, 123, 154
Columbia River Treaty, 74, 122
communications. *See* microwave telecommunication system
Congress (BC), 118, 149
Consolidated Railway and Light Company, 10, 11
Cotton, Barry, 25
Creeden, Flossie, 76
Cunningham, Charlie, 150
Curry family, 118

D

Dakelh (Carrier) people, 40
dances, 137, 142
Davidson, Big Bill, 54, 117, 149–50
Dawson Wade Construction, 61
Declaration of the Lillooet Tribe, 42–43
deer, xiii, *172*
de Hullu, Emma, 32
Depression, xi, 27, 31, 32, 33, 54, 125
Devine (BC), 67
Devine sawmill, 65, 67
Devitt, Dave, 58, 126, *127*, 128–29
Devitt, Dean, 128
Devitt, Jack, 58, 126
Devitt, Phil, 128
Devitt family, 58, 60, 126, 127, 130
De Yagher, Corinne, 135, 137, 147, *147*

De Yagher, Dennis, 87, 135, *136*, 144–45, 146, 147, *147*
Dillon, Remmy, *157*
Dinner for Miss Creeden (film), 76–77
divers, deep-sea, *82–83*, 83–84, 118, *118*
Douglas, James, 41–42
Downey, Ross, *136*, 137, *138*, *139*, 142, 144
Downey, Vicki, *138*, 144
Downton, Geoffrey: background, 5; at Bridge River opening ceremonies, 102, *103*, 120; initial development of Bridge River, 5, 6; original vision for Bridge River, 3, 4, 49, 175; St'át'imc Nation and, 39; in WWI, 6
Downton Lake Reservoir, 9, 45, 88, 89, 173, 177
Drake-Terry, Joanne, 43
Dunham, Dr., 64
Durban, Frank, 24

E

East and West Kootenay Power and Light, 78
East Lillooet (BC), 56, 62, 65, 66
Edison, Thomas, 7
education: elementary grades, 143–44; high school, 144–45; Japanese Canadian internees and, 60, 127; original Bridge River school, 60, 128, *129*; residential schools, 43–44; Sk'il' Mountain Community School, *172*; teachers, 142–43, 144
Edwards, Irene and Bill, 118
Edwards, Michelle, 170
Eldorado Mountain, 117
electricity, 3–4, 7. *See also* Bridge River power project; hydroelectricity; thermal electricity

185

Elsinga, Mike, *168*
emergency spills, 158–62, 177–78
engineers, xiv–xv, 4, 5
Enjo, Den, 62
environment: Carpenter Lake Reservoir cleanup efforts, 151–53; emergency spills, 158–62, 177–78; fish stocks, 46–47, 153–57, 162; impacts from Bridge River project, xiii; land encroachment on St'át'imc Nation, 51, 158; land flooded by Carpenter Lake Reservoir, 149, 150–51; retreating glaciers, 164–65; Seton Lake changes, 47; thermal power projects and, 121; Water Use Planning Program, 162–63, 165
Evans, Curly, 32
Evans, Neil, 62
Evans Transport, 32, *33*
Evenden, Matthew, 5, 72, 73, 75, 100, 155

F

Finney, Glen, 145
First World War, 6, 24, 27
Fisheries Act, 161
fish stocks, 46–47, 153–57, 162. *See also* salmon
Fleming, Owen, 160
flooding, 73–74, 100, 149, 150–51. *See also* emergency spills
floorman, 131
Fort Peck Dam (Montana), 80–81
Foster, W.W., 22
Fourneyron, Benoît, 36
Fox, Clifford, 57
Francis, James, 36–37
Francis reaction turbines, 36–37, 95
Frank, Brian, *156*
Frank, Pricilla, *156*
Fraser, Simon, ix, 40

Fraser Canyon Gold Rush (1858), 40–41, 43. *See also* gold
Fraser River, 44, 46, 100, 116, 154, 155. *See also* Seton power project
Fujiwara, Alan, 58, 147
Fujiwara, Asajiro, 58, 147

G

Gage, A.W.G., 22
Gage, Walter, 22, 56
Gaglardi, Phil, 24
Galloway, J.D., 14, *17*, 19, 28
gas, natural, 34, 76, 108, 112, 175
Gay, George, and family, 60
Geen, G.H., 154
Gemmill, Jim, *36*, *138*, 142
Gemmill, Susan, *138*, 142, 144
glaciers, retreating, 164–65
gold, ix, 9, 32, 40–42, 43, 125, 149
Gold, Kerry, *36*, *168*
Goldstream power plant, 16
Gomer Sunahara, Ann, 53
Gordon, Walter, 34
Grauer, Albert Edward "Dal": ambitions for Bridge River project, 34, 77, 103–5, 128; background, 34; at Bridge River opening ceremony, 101, 102; death, 123; *Dinner for Miss Creeden* (film) and, 76; leadership of BC Electric, 34, 35, 71, 76, 128; Masajiro Miyazaki and, 56, 65; against Peace and Columbia Rivers development, 122; Public Information department and, 75
Great Depression, xi, 27, 31, 32, 33, 54, 125
Grosvenor Group, 115
grout curtain, 82–83, 84
Grumman Goose aircraft, 24, *26*

H

Haida, 41
Hamilton, James, 41
Hart, John, 75, 78
Hat Creek coal deposits, 121, 122, 154
Hayward Lake Reservoir, 15
Heinrich, Bob, 133, *133*, 134
Heinrich, Herbert, 60, 126
Heinrich, Jack, 134
Heinrich, John, 60, *87*, 126, *133*, 134, *135*
Heinrich, Wally, 134
Hell's Gate, 153
Hendrickson, Otto, 57–58
Hendry, John, 13, 14
Highline Road, 170
Hildebrand, Ben, 130–31
Holt, Herbert S., 26, 27
Holtby, Bill, 136
Homemakers (BCER radio show), 31–32
Hood, Ken, 141, 144
Horne-Payne, Robert Montgomery, 10–12, *11*, 13, 14, 27, 41, 76
Horne Payne substation, 112
Horsefly River, 40
horses, wild, 62
Horton, Phil, 76–77
Horton, Phyllis, 76–77
Houghton, Fred, 99
Howe, C.D., 72–73
Hudson's Bay Company, ix, 40, 41
Hughes, Mr. (teacher), 60
Hume & Rumble electrical company, 97, 134
Hunt, Chester, 126
Hurley, Chuck, *136*
hydroelectricity, 3, 12, 73–75. *See also* Alouette Lake power project; Bridge River power project; Buntzen Lake power project; Columbia River power project; Jordan River hydroelectric project;

Lajoie Dam and powerhouse; Peace River power project; Ruskin power project; Stave Lake (Stave Falls) power project; turbine technology; Walden North hydroelectric project

I

impulse turbine (Pelton wheel), *36, 37,* 94, *94,* 95, 175
Indian Act (1876), 39, 42
Indigenous peoples: BC Hydro and, 168, 169; donation for Lillooet ambulance, 65; gold rushes and, 40, 41-42, 43; Indian Act and, 39, 42; Masajiro Miyazaki and, 63-64; reserves, 42, 158; residential schools, 43-44. *See also* St'át'imc Nation; *other First Nations*
Ingledow, Tom, 65, 95, 101-2
Ingledow substation, 112
International Pacific Salmon Fisheries Commission, 154
internment. *See* Japanese Canadian internment
interurban transit system, 13, 14, 71, 108. *See also* bus transit system; streetcars
irrigation, 13, 65, 113-14, *114*
Irvine, H., *17*

J

jade, *87*
Japanese Canadian internment, 53-55, 56-57, 60-61, 62, 65, 66-67, 68, 127. *See also* Miyazaki, Masajiro
Joe, Wing, 160
John, Darwyn, 46-48
John, Garry (Qwalqwalten), *163*
John Hart Dam and powerhouse, 105
Jones Lake (Wahleach) power station, 113

Jordan River hydroelectric project, 13, 33
J.W. Stewart Limited, 77, 101

K

Kaminishi, Koichi, 62
Kaoham Shuttle, 145, *145,* 173
Keatley Creek archaeological site, 49, *50*
Keenleyside, Hugh, 123
kekuli holes (pit houses), 49-51, *50*
Kelsch, Raymond S., 16-18, 94
Kemano (BC), 76
Kenney, E.T., 74
Kenney Dam (formerly Nechako River Dam), 74
Kidd, George: background, 13; BC Electric's jubilee and, 76; Bralorne mine and, 32; Bridge River development and, 14, 16, 18, 19, 27, 28; at Ruskin power plant opening ceremony, 31
Kidd substation, 112
Kido, Mr. (teacher), 60
Killam, Izaak Walton, 7
Kitimat (BC), 76
Klit, Paul, 81, 82, 83

L

Lacroix, Yves, 84, 87, 118, 119-20, *120*
Lajoie, Joseph Zotique (Lazack), 8-9
Lajoie Dam and powerhouse: about, x, 9; construction, *88,* 88-89, *89,* 90, 105, 115; costs, 112; Downton Lake Reservoir and, 45; rehabilitation, 173, 177-78; view from, *150*
Lajoie Falls, 8-9, 33
Lajoie Lake (Little Gun Lake), 9
Lambert, Noel, 102
Lamperson, G.W., 162
lamps, carbide, 25

land encroachment, 51, 158
Langley control centre, xi, 146
Lavigne, Harvey, 134, *136*
Lavigne, Joyce, 134
Lazenby, Eric, *17*
Lazenby, F.A., 80, 86
Legge, Ralph, 159-60
Lighted Journey (Maiden), 75, 77
Lillooet (BC), 3, 32, 41, *61,* 61-63, 64-65. *See also* East Lillooet
Lillooet people, 42. *See also* St'át'imc Nation
Lillooet School Board, 145
Lil'tem' Mountain Hotel (Seton Portage), *169,* 169-70
Lil'wat (Mount Currie) Band, 49
Little Gun Lake (Lajoie Lake), 10
Louie, Candace, *48*
Louie, Rod, *50,* 158, *168,* 170, 173
Lytton (BC), 63, 66

M

Mackenzie, William, 7
Maiden, Cecil, 12, 16, 21, 31, 76, 77; *Lighted Journey,* 75, 77
Mainwaring, W.C., 101-2
Malkin, William, 31
Mann, Donald, 7
Mawson, Thomas, 5-6
McBrayne, Mr., 61
McGeachy family, 60
McGillivray Falls (BC), 56
McKay, Bill, 137, *139,* 141
McLeod, S.M., 21
McStay, Bud, *99*
Merilees, Harold, 75
Michel, Gerald, 45-46, 165
microwave telecommunication system, 59, 125, 136, *141,* 142
Miller, Michael, 83
Minto City (BC), xiii, 24, 53-54, 56, 59, 66, 117-18, 149

Mission Dam. *See* Terzaghi Dam
Mission Mountain: bobsledding down, 138, *139*, 141; hiking on, 133, *133*; microclimate, x; microwave and television antennae, 136, *140*, *141*; name of, 45; road over, 21; snow camp, 59; tunnels through, xi, 90, *91*
Mitchell, Gerald, *50*
Miyazaki, Betty, 57, 65
Miyazaki, Ken, 56-57, 62, 67
Miyazaki, Masajiro: ambulance service and, 64-65; background, 56; family home and doctor's office in Lillooet, 62, 63, *66*, 67; Indigenous peoples and, 63-64; internment in Bridge River, 55, 56, 57-58, 60; move to Lillooet, 61-63; photograph, *57*; postwar life, 67; snow camp and, 59
Miyazaki, Rumiko, 56
Miyazaki House (Lillooet), 62, 63, *66*, 67
Moha Road, *23*, 24, *87*, 129, 133
Molstad, Terry, *163*
Montreal Light, Heat & Power, 72
Montreal syndicates, 6-7, 14, 16, 26
Moran Canyon, 154
Murray, George, 68-69
Murray, Margaret "Ma," 67, 68-69, *69*
Murrin, William George (W.G.): background, 13; BC Electric's jubilee and, 76; on Great Depression, 33, 35; Japanese Canadian internment and, 54, 127; leadership of BC Electric, 27; retirement, 71, 128; at Ruskin power plant opening ceremony, 31
Murrin substation, 112

N
Napoleon, Tom, 119
natural gas, 34, 76, 108, 112, 175
Nechako River Dam (later Kenney Dam), 74
Nelless, Audrey, 142
Nelless, Bob, *136*, *138*, 142
Nesbitt, Arthur, 7, 26
Nesbitt, Thomson & Company, 7, 26
New Brighton Park (Brighton Beach, Vancouver), 29
New Deal, 73
Newell, J.I., 15, 27-28
nitrogen fertilizer, 13
Nlaka'pamux (Thompson) people, 49
Northern Construction Company, 77, 101, 102
North West Company, ix
N'Quatqua (Anderson Lake) Band, 49

O
O'Kelly, Fred, *136*
Oleman, Patrick, 21, 138
Oliver, John, 56
Olsen (constable), 60
Olsen, Edgar, *136*, *138*
Olsen, Mark, 87
Ontario, 71, 73, 74-75
O'Riley, Chris, xiii, 158, 165, 168, 169
Osborne, Brenda, 135-36
Osborne, Dennis, 135-36, *140*, 142

P
Pacific Engineering, 22
Pacific Great Eastern (PGE) Railway: about, 60; Budd Car, 24, *25*, 128-29, 131, 134, 135, 142, 144-45; Cayoosh Creek power plant, 61; donation for Lillooet ambulance, 65; employment with, 51, 61; land encroachment upon St'át'imc, 158; Shalalth station (Bridge River townsite), 21, 32, 33; travel to and from Bridge River via, 3, 24, 65, 101, 129-30, *130*, 131, 142. *See also* BC Rail
Pacific Salmon Treaty, 157
Paddy (Minto hotel owner), 117
Parry, Lew, 76
Parry, Malcolm, *81*, 84, 119-20, 130
Patterson, Dr., 61, 63
Paul, Emily, 51
Paul, Francis, 51
Peace River Power Development Company, 120, 154
Peace River power project: Bennett and, 74, 121, 122, 154; development of, 120, 154; Site C, xi, 175; transmission lines for, 123; turbines, 95
Pelton, Lester, 37
Pelton wheel (impulse turbine), *36*, 37, 94, *94*, 95, 175
penstocks, 4, 92, 93, *93*, 109, 170, *171*
Peter, Ida Mary, 45, 170
Peter, Mission, 45
Phair, Artie, 62-63, 67
Phair, Caspar and Cerise, 62
Phair, Harold, 62, 63
piezometers, 83
pilings, sheet, 83-84, *85*, 118
pink salmon, 153, 154, *155*, 157. *See also* salmon
Pioneer mine, 24, 32, 42, 71, 131
pit houses (kekuli holes), 49-51, *50*
Polischuk, Paul, 152-53
Port Douglas (BC), 158, 167
Post-War Rehabilitation Council, 72, 74-75, 78, 105
Powell River (BC), 115
Powell River News, 115
Powell River Pulp and Paper, 28
Power Corporation. *See* BC Power Corporation

Power Corporation of Canada, 7, 26
powerhouses: construction of, 94–96, *96*, 120; photographs, *35*, *94–95*, *96*, *111*, *174*, *177*; rehabilitation efforts, 175–76, *177*; stabilization efforts, 110–11, *111*; temporary powerhouse, xi, 33, *35*, 60, 125–26
Prince George (BC), 123
Prince Rupert (BC), 76
pulp and paper industry, 7, 13, 28, 76
Purchas, John, 26
Purney, Harry, 133, *133*, 137, *137*, 144
Purney, Nina, 137, *137*
Purney, Rob, 137, 144
Purves, Ralph, 28

Q

Quebec, 17, 72
Quirk, Ed, 102
Qwalqwalten (Garry John), *163*

R

radio: *Homemakers* show, 31–32
railway: Budd Car, 24, *25*, 128–29, 131, 134, 135, 142, 144–45; Kaoham Shuttle, 145, *145*, 173. *See also* Pacific Great Eastern (PGE) Railway
reaction turbines, Francis, 36–37, 95
Read, John R., 7
Redan, Perry, 43–44, 49, 173
reserves, Indigenous, 42, 158
residential schools, 43–44
Rexmount (BC), 149
Rexworthy, E., 17
Ripley, Charles F., 87
Riverland Irrigated Farm, 114, *114*
roads: early development, 125; Highline Road, 170; keeping open in winter, 59; Moha Road, *23*, 24, 87, 129, 133; over Mission Mountain, 21; transmission line access roads, 99
Rock Bay bridge collapse (Victoria), 11, *12*
Rogers, Jonathan, 5
Rogers Building (Vancouver), 4–5
Roosevelt, Franklin D., 73
Ross, Bert, 134
Ross, Holly, 134
Ross, Ken, 134
Royal Commission on Canada's Economic Prospects, 34
Royal Securities Corporation, 7, 14
rural communities, 74–75, 78
Ruskin power project: Bridge River project and, 16, 27, 28, 29, 30, 71; development of, 15, 29, 31; Devitt family at, 130; power generation, 31, 72, 94, 112. *See also* Alouette Lake power project; Stave Lake (Stave Falls) power project
Russell, Bill, 134

S

Sahlins, Marshall, 39
Saimoto, Ritsu, 54–55, 66–67
salmon: Bridge River project impacts, xiii, 46–47; conservation efforts, 48, 153–54, *155*, *156*, 157, *157*, 162, *163*; emergency spills and, 158–62; glaciers and, 165; gold prospecting impacts, 41; St'át'imc Nation and, 44–45, *45*, 46, 46–47, *47*, 48, *48*, 49
Samahquam First Nation, 49, 167
school. *See* education
Scotchman, Isis, *48*
Scotchman, Jimmy, 119
Scouras, Jim, 173
scow, at Seton Lake, 24
Seaman Paper Company, 28
Second World War, 27, 35, 37, 53. *See also* Japanese Canadian internment
Sekw'el'was (Cayoose Creek) Band, 44, 49, 157, 170
Sepwecemc (Shuswap) people, 40, 49
Seton Lake: about, x; Bridge River project impacts, 47; freezing of, 138, *139*; glacial water in, 164; pulp mill proposal, 28; scow, 24; water skiing, *132*, 133
Seton Portage, x, 118, 134, 136, 170
Seton power project: emergency spills, 161; fish ladder and salmon conservation, 48, 153, 154, *155*, 157; generation plant, x–xi, xii, 33, 115–16; map, *106–7*; photographs, *108*, *109*; rehabilitation, 176
Shalalth (BC), x, 24, 32, 33, 41, 47, 55. *See also* Bridge River (townsite)
Shalalth General Store, 60
Shaw, Angus, ix
Shawinigan Engineering Company, 77, 81
sheet pilings, 83–84, *85*, 118
Shepherd, Jim, 111, 170, 178
Shields, Clara, 144
Shields, Fran, *172*
Shields, Fred, 119
Shields-Joseph, Veronica, *172*
Shrum, Gordon, 123
Simpson, Barbara, 143–44
Site C (Peace River), xi, 175
Skatin (Skookumchuck) First Nation, 49, 167
Sk'il' Mountain Community School, *172*
Smeaton, John, 36
Smith, Hugh, 161, 162–63, 165
Smith, J. Fyfe, 5
snow camp, 59
sockeye salmon, 153, 154, 157. *See also* salmon
Soletanche, 84

South Shalalth (BC), x, 60. *See also* Bridge River (townsite)
Spences Bridge (BC), 113
Sperling, R.H., 14
Sperling and Company, 10
spills, emergency, 158-62, 177-78
St'át'imc Chiefs Council, 167, 170
St'át'imc Nation: agreements with BC Hydro, 167-70, 173; Bridge River project impacts on, xi, xv, 51; Bridge River Valley and, ix-x; Declaration of the Lillooet Tribe, 42-43; Downton's survey trip and, 39; economic development, 169-70, 173; education and, 64, 143-44, 145, *172*; first encounters with white men, 40; gold rushes and, 42, 43; land encroachment and, 51, 158; Moha Trail, 24; peace with Tsilhqot'in, 40; pit houses (kekuli holes), 49-51, *50*; population, 49; residential schools and, 43-44; salmon and, xiii, 44-47, *45*, *46*, *47*, 48, *48*, 49, 157; Terzaghi (Mission) Dam and, 48; traditional way of life, 39, 42, 44, 49. *See also* Indigenous peoples
Stave Lake Power Company (later Western Power Company of Canada), 7, 13, 14-15
Stave Lake (Stave Falls) power project: Bridge River project and, 22, 164; development of, 15; employment at, 126, 134; power generation, 31; rivalry over, 14. *See also* Alouette Lake power project; Ruskin power project
Steede, Jack, 28-29, 37, 95
Stewart, Mel, *88*, 114, 116-19, 149-50, 153, 159, 160, 161-62
Stone & Webster engineering and utilities company, 14

Strang, Mr. (Indian Agent), 63
Strategic Fisheries Project, 162. *See also* fish stocks; salmon
streetcars, 11, 12, 13, 32, 77, 116. *See also* bus transit system; interurban transit system
substations, Greater Vancouver, 112
Sunahara, Ann Gomer. *See* Gomer Sunahara, Ann
surveyors and surveying, xiv-xv, 3, 4, 5, *81*, 116, 117
Swanson, Cecil, 102
Swoboda, Don: on Carpenter Lake Reservoir cleanup, 153; on emergency spills, 161; on life in Bridge River, 133, *134*; photographs, *133*, *168*; on powerhouses, 94, 95, 110; on snow camp, 59; on Terzaghi (Mission) Dam, 80
Syilx (Okanagan) people, 49

T

Takahashi, Miss (teacher), 60
Takimoto, Yojiro, 65
Tattersall, Peter, 153
Taylor, Austin C., 32, 53, 54, 56
telecommunications, microwave system, 59, 125, 136, *141*, 142
television, 136, *140*
tennis club, *129*, 134
Terzaghi, Karl, 30, 80, 81, 82-83, 84, 86-87, 110, 118
Terzaghi, Ruth Doggett, 80, 87
Terzaghi Dam (formerly Mission Dam), 79-87; Carpenter Lake Reservoir and, 45; completion, 106; construction challenges and leak fears, 22, 30, 80-81; construction relaunched post-WWII, 78, *79*, *79*, 80, *80*; emergency spills, 158-62; impacts on Bridge River, xiii; Indigenous peoples and, 48; land flooded by, 149; Ma Murray and, 69; Moha Road and, 24; old pilings removed by deep-sea divers, 82-83, 83-84, 118, *118*; original diversion dam, 22, 79, 81; rehabilitation and grout curtain, 82-83, 84; salmon conservation and permanent water release, 162, *163*, *168*; seal over, *117*, 118; sheet pilings, 84, *85*; spillway, 84, *86*; surveying work, *81*; as Terzaghi's legacy, 86-87
Tesla, Nikola, 7
Texada Island, 115
thermal electricity: about, 12; BC Energy Plan and, 121; Burrard Thermal plant, 120, 123, 134, 135; Hat Creek coal deposits and, 121, 122, 154; proposed plant at Brighton Beach, 29
Thomas, E., 33
Thompson, Peter, 26
Thompson, Walter, 141
Thompson River region, 113-14
Tingley, Steve, 41
Tipella Creek, 158
T'it'q'et (Lillooet) Band, 49
Tolmie, S.F., 31
Tom, John, 21
tourism, *169*, 173
transit. *See* bus transit system; interurban transit system
transmission lines: construction and expansion, xiv, 97, *97*, 99, *99*, 108, 112, 113, 116, 123; land encroachment and, 158; photographs, *98*, *113*
Trans Mountain Oil Pipe Line Company, 76
Tsal'alh (Seton Lake) Band, x, 44, 49, 145, 170, *172*
Tsilhqot'in (Chilcotin) people, x, 40, 49
Tskw'aylaxw (Pavilion) Band, 49

tunnel construction, 21–23, 25, 26, 29, 31, 90, *91*
Tupper, Charles Hibbert, 13, 14
turbine technology, 36–37, 94, *94*, 95
"Two Rivers Policy," 122, 154–55

U

United States of America, 15, 73–74, 112, 154
University of British Columbia, 56

V

Vancouver, 6, 13, 31, 73
Vancouver Daily Province, 16
Vancouver Daily Sun, 28
Vancouver Iron and Engineering Works, 93
Vancouver Island, 13, 34, 105, 112, 116
Vancouver Power Company, 12, 23
Vancouver Sun, 100, 130
Van Horne, William, 10
Vaughn, H.T., 7
Victoria (BC), 11, *12*, 41
Victoria Electric Railway and Lighting Company, 11

W

Wahleach (Jones Lake) power station, 113
Walden North hydroelectric project, 170
Walters, Howard, 75
Warren, Harry, 74
Water Act, 8–9
Water Clauses Consolidation Act (1897), 12
water skiing, *132*, 133

Water Use Planning Program, 162–63, 165
water wheel, 36. *See also* turbine technology
Wayside (BC), 118, 149
Weber, Frank, 164–65
Wenner-Gren, Axel, 122
Western Development and Power Limited, 116
Western Power Company of Canada (WPCC; formerly Western Canada Power Company, Stave Lake Power Company), 7, 13, 14–15
Westinghouse, 7
Weston, S.R., 102–3
Williams, Adolphus, 5–6
Williams, John, 5
Wilson, Pat, 142–43
Winch, Harold E., 74
Wittnauer, Longines, 84
World War I, 6, 24, 27
World War II, 27, 35, 37, 53. *See also* Japanese Canadian internment

X

Xaxli'p (Fountain) First Nation, 49
Xa'xtsa (Douglas) First Nation, 49, 167
Xwisten (Bridge River) Band, 44, 49, 50–51, 168

Y

Yada, George, 60
Yada, Ken, 54, 67
Yada family, 54, 67
Yada's general store (Lillooet), 24, 60, 67, 130, 134
Young, Harry, 123